basic
BASI

Second Editi

Donald M Monro

Edward Arnold
A division of Hodder & Stoughton

LONDON   MELBOURNE   AUCKLAND

© 1985 Donald M Monro

First published in Great Britain 1978
Reprinted 1979, 1980, 1981 (twice), 1982, 1984
Second edition 1985
Reprinted 1988, 1989

British Library Cataloguing in Publication Data

Monro, Donald M.
   Basic BASIC.——2nd ed.
   1. Basic (Computer program language)
   I. Title
   001.64′24   QA76.73.B3

ISBN 0 7131 3533 6

For Douglas

Printed and bound in Great Britain for Edward Arnold, the educational, academic and medical publishing division of Hodder and Stoughton Limited, 41 Bedford Square, London WC1B 3DQ by J. W. Arrowsmith Ltd, Bristol

PREFACE

Computer programming is something that nearly everyone can do, and many people are now finding this out using BASIC, the language designed to help them learn. The second edition of this little course again gives priority to two objectives which I believe are necessary in the learning process. First of all it is fully structured, which means that I intend it to be followed in order using a computer. (I am flattered by the extent to which this principle, almost unique at the time of the first edition, has been imitated.) Secondly I feel that the level of examples and problems must be neither so banal as to insult the intelligence of the reader, nor so advanced as to be bewildering. I recognise that practical computing cannot be totally non-mathematical —after all it is numbers that are dealt with—and so some of the material is related to secondary school mathematics. There are also some instances of numerical computation which I hope will be regarded from a programming point of view rather than a mathematical one. All the material is intended to be approachable.

This book describes the basic BASIC that everyone should know. I can say this for sure because international standards for 'minimal BASIC' have now been adopted which are very close to the basic BASIC that I originally chose, and the second edition is intended to be in harmony with the standard. Because of the recent explosive growth in home and educational computers, I hope the new edition will continue to meet the need for an introduction to the subset of BASIC that one could reasonably expect to find on any small computer.

You see before you the first attempt at using a new interactive computer system for typesetting which James Murphy has worked very hard at realising for me over the past eighteen months. This book is proof of its success, and my editor Jan Williams has been particularly courageous in using it to set up *basic BASIC* while it was still at the 'User Hostile' stage of development. I extend my heartfelt thanks to both of you. There is also a special medal of honour for David James who has volunteered to spend part if not all of his Christmas holiday hacking through the examples one last time on his BBC Micro, to reduce if not eliminate the risk that our dear readers may have to cope with the dreaded typographical errors in the programs.

This new edition takes account of the new importance of desk- and table-top computing, and I have managed to squeeze additional examples of small programs that will work into nearly every chapter. Apart from that, I have hardly dared to tamper with such a successful formula. I hope that this little book will continue to meet the needs of so many schools, colleges and private citizens.

Completed on Christmas Eve 1984

D M Monro

Contents

INTRODUCTION

1 Computer languages

Like any language, BASIC is used by people for the communication of ideas. Unlike English, French, or German, a communication in BASIC is directed towards a calculating machine which is somehow equipped to accept instructions written in BASIC. There are many computer languages, some intended for specific uses and others which are said to be general, meaning that any computing task could be expressed using them. BASIC is at the same time both specific and general, and more people now use it than any other computer language. The name BASIC stands for 'Beginner's All-purpose Symbolic Instruction Code', and the word 'beginners' is the key to its special use as a language for learning the fundamentals of computation in an easily understood form. Perhaps that is why it is the standard language of so many small computers, and in turn that is why so many people are now using it. At the same time BASIC is a very useful general purpose language with some unique features.

All languages have rules of grammar, and in computing these rules must be precise so that no statement of the language has more than one meaning. However, BASIC has a grammar which is intentionally simplified so that only a few rules must be learned before real computations can be performed, as will be seen in Unit 1. Because all the essential facilities for computation are present, the emphasis can be placed on the style and methods of computation. When the techniques of computing have been mastered it is easy to convert to the traditional languages of large scale computation because BASIC strongly resembles them.

2 Computer systems

Every computer is organised around a calculating machine which might be a single microchip, or a huge system. Such a machine has no personality or intelligence of its own; anything it does is a result of human instruction. It has a repertoire of simple orders which it obeys slavishly. A series of these orders would be called a computer program; the concept of a program is an easy one for humans to grasp and develops naturally in this course by example. It is important to realise that the machine cannot tell if its very literal interpretation of the program makes sense. A computer's mistakes are nearly always the fault of the program.

3 Batch and interactive computing

Originally computer systems were organised to deal with one program at a time, and programs were presented in groups or 'batches' which the machine processed one after the other. The programmer submitted his program to a computing service, usually on punched cards, and collected the result some time later. BASIC, like any other language, can be run in this way, and a great deal of computing is still done in batches. The disadvantage for small programs and for learning is that the 'turnaround' time is unlikely to be less than a few hours and could be measured in days. However batch systems are very widely used, particularly for production work, for reasons of economy.

Recently, the cost of computers has fallen and at the same time their capabilities have increased. Now a personal computer, dedicated to one user, is a common sight at work, in the classroom and in the homes of ordinary people. This means that 'interactive computing' is now available to nearly everyone.

Interactive computing puts a programmer into direct communication with the computer, usually through a terminal with a keyboard and a screen or typewriter. He may have the computer to himself or he may be 'timesharing' with others unseen to him. The time taken to submit a program and receive results is reduced to seconds and so program development and error correction are supported in a convenient manner. The learning process is both shortened and made more thorough because the rapid response and the straighforward nature of BASIC encourage experimentation.

4 How to learn BASIC

The key to effective learning is practice on a real computer. First of all, it is essential to be able to run BASIC programs, ideally by using an interactive system. A source of expert advice is required, not so much about BASIC as about your computer system. To learn BASIC simply follow the Units in order and do all the exercises because they provide exploration and clarification which are vital to complete understanding. If there is something that is not clear to you, then experiment using BASIC. That is the joy of interactive computing. Problems are provided at the end of each Unit. Solutions to problems should be worked out on paper before trying them at a terminal. Nothing is more futile than trying to think out solutions at the keyboard; even the most tentative outline can save hours.

UNIT 1
Getting started

1 Introduction

An advantage of BASIC is that a small amount of information enables it to be used. This makes it easy to learn and easy to remember. This Unit introduces the simplest kind of BASIC program and shows how to create, edit, and run it.

2 A simple program in BASIC—the PRINT and END statements

A computer program in BASIC is a series of instructions having a natural order, written as *statements* using familiar English and mathematical terms. The meaning of the program is clear to the programmer and is also precise for the computer.

The following very simple BASIC program has two lines, each stating an instruction to the computer from the programmer:

```
1Ø PRINT 2+2
2Ø END
```

The program instructs the computer to evaluate the *expression* $2+2$ and to print the result. Two important grammatical rules of BASIC are evident in the example:

(i) Each of the two lines begins with a *line number*. These line numbers dictate the order of events when a program is obeyed. Every line must begin with a line number.

(ii) The program ends with an END statement. Every BASIC program should have an END statement as its highest numbered line. Although some computers allow it to be left out, a BASIC like that is not standard.

Two different statements of BASIC appear in this simple example, the PRINT statement and the END statement. The intention of the program is clear; when it is obeyed by a computer, at line 10 a sum $(2+2)$ is evaluated and at line 20 the program ends.

The meaning of complicated programs can often be clarified by the use of a flowchart, which shows diagrammatically the steps involved in a computer program and their order. This simple program has a simple flowchart, as shown in Fig. 1.1.

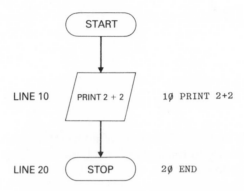

Fig. 1.1. Flowchart of a very simple BASIC program

3   Creating BASIC programs

A BASIC program is created simply by typing it at the computer keyboard. Most computers that use BASIC are based on *interactive* use, where the programmer communicates directly with the computer through a keyboard. This is true both of huge timesharing computers with hundreds of terminals and of the humblest home computer dedicated to its proud owner. Large computers have their own procedures for recognising permitted users and connecting them to interactive BASIC. This is where expert help may be required for the first time.

With the computer system prepared to receive a program, the little program given above can be entered by typing it. The keyboard is laid out very much like a typewriter but some of the special symbols such as ' + ' are in unexpected places and there are some extra keys. Each separate line is entered, beginning with its line number and ending with the special key used to terminate lines. Usually this key is labelled 'RETURN', but sometimes it is 'ENTER'. It is always at the right hand end of the keyboard. The first symbols typed must be the line number. The order in which the lines are entered is unimportant because the line numbers tell BASIC what the real order should be. It is usual to separate the line numbers by 10, since the programmer may later wish to insert extra lines, although any separation is allowed down to consecutive numbers. At least one space is usually required after the line number. Keywords like PRINT and END must have either spaces or punctuation on both sides of them.

Exercise   With the computer system ready for it, enter the simple program. Be careful that the first symbols in each line are the line number. Do not begin a line with a space, and do not attempt to correct errors at this stage.

4 Listing BASIC programs—the command LIST

Typing mistakes can easily occur in entering a BASIC program, and errors between the computer and the keyboard are possible, although unlikely. Once a program has been entered it is important to be able to examine it as it is known to the computer. The system command LIST is usually provided for this purpose, and causes the current version of the program to be displayed on the screen or terminal.

Exercise Use the command LIST to obtain a listing of the sample program.

It is important to distinguish between commands like LIST whose first symbol is a letter, and lines of BASIC which begin with a number. This is how the computer tells the difference; everything that begins with a number is a line of BASIC.

5 Editing BASIC programs

It is very likely that typing or other mistakes will be made when a program is entered, so that a means of editing is necessary. With BASIC it is possible to change lines, insert new lines, and eliminate unwanted ones. All these procedures are based on the line numbers; when a new line is typed in it becomes a part of the program. The procedures are:

(i) To replace or correct a line: type the new line in full and press 'RETURN'.

Example The program reads

```
1Ø  PRANT  2+2
2Ø  END
```

You type in

```
1Ø  PRINT  2+2  and 'RETURN'
```

The corrected program reads

```
1Ø  PRINT  2+2
2Ø  END
```

(ii) To insert a line: type in the new line with a suitable line number and 'RETURN'. For example a new line numbered 15 could be inserted between lines 10 and 20 of the sample program.

Example To the sample program you add a line by typing

```
15  PRINT  5+3
```

The program then reads

```
10  PRINT  2+2
15  PRINT  5+3
20  END
```

(iii) To eliminate a line: type in only the line number, and 'RETURN'.

Example   To delete the extra line added in (ii) you type

```
15   (just the line number and 'RETURN'
      with no blank spaces)
```

The program then reads

```
10  PRINT  2+2
20  END
```

Note that to correct a line, the new version has to be typed in full. This is sometimes tedious, so that careful original typing is always worthwhile. Most systems also provide a means of correcting characters in a line while it is being typed. On the keyboard there will be a symbol which deletes the previous one—a letter gobbling key. Often this is a '←' ('back arrow') but sometimes it is DEL or backspace or CTRL and H. Ask an expert. An incorrect symbol in any program line or command which is noticed before the line is finished can be removed by typing in enough of these letter gobblers to reach the error, and then typing of the line can be resumed from the corrected symbol. For example the twice corrected line

```
10  PRA←INP  2+2←←←←←T  2+2
```

is the same as

```
10  PRINT  2+2
```

In the version with back arrows, the blank betwen P and 2 counts as a character.

Exercise   Experiment with the editing facilities to add, change, and delete lines in the sample program. Find out what the letter gobbler is on your computer, and try using it to correct errors while typing. Finally, restore the program to its given form and list it to be sure.

6   Running BASIC programs—the command RUN

So far in this Unit the sample program has been created, listed, and edited, but it has not been tried. The command RUN is provided to initiate the running of a program. When the RUN command is entered, the computer begins to execute the instructions given by the program. When a program is running the computer has taken control of the session and it is not possible to edit the program or to use other commands until it is finished. The sample program will terminate itself at the END statement.

Exercise Run the sample program, by typing in the command RUN.

7 Problems

Problem 1.1 The following BASIC program has been entered. Is it correct?

```
2Ø PRINP 1+3
1Ø END
```

Without using the computer, try to follow what happens to the program as the following lines are typed in order. RETURN is pressed after each line:

(i)	3Ø END	(v)	25 PRINT 5−3
(ii)	1Ø	(vi)	2Ø PRIYP⇐⇐NT 1+3
(iii)	15	(vii)	2PR⇐⇐5
(iv)	2Ø PRINT 1P3	(viii)	LIST

Is it now correct? What will happen if the RUN command is entered? So try it.

Problem 1.2 The computer will interpret the following lines as either lines of BASIC or commands. Classify them as one or the other from the computer's point of view. The symbol ⇐⇐ stands for the letter gobbling key.

(i)	1Ø PRINT 3	(v)	PRINT 2+2
(ii)	LIST	(vi)	15 LIST
(iii)	2Ø⇐⇐END	(vii)	99⇐⇐RUN
(iv)	RUN⇐⇐⇐3Ø END	(viii)	LIST⇐⇐⇐4Ø END

Not all of these lines will produce a correct line of BASIC. Which are correct?

UNIT 2

The arithmetic of BASIC

1 Introduction

Armed with the ability to prepare simple BASIC programs acquired in Unit 1, it is now possible to introduce the rules of arithmetic as they apply to BASIC. By the end of this unit it will be possible to use BASIC on your computer as a programmable calculator for the evaluation of complicated expressions.

2 Addition and subtraction

The sample program of Unit 1 included the addition facility. An expression including addition is formed simply by placing a plus sign between the numbers to be added. In the expressions considered here the numbers are constants like 1, 2, 3, etc., and expressions are formed from these. The program

```
1Ø PRINT 2+2
2Ø END
```

contains the *expression* 2+2 formed by the *operation* of addition between the *constants* 2 and 2. A number by itself is an expression as well, such as in

```
1Ø PRINT 35
2Ø END
```

Not surprisingly the operation of subtraction is indicated by a minus sign:

```
1Ø PRINT 4−3
2Ø END
```

Everyone knows that the order of addition is unimportant; that is, 5+1 is the same as 1+5. This is not true for subtraction, since 5−1 is not the same as 1−5. This is an obvious example of an important fact, namely that the order of numbers and operators like + and − in an expression is important. In BASIC the results always appear as if the operations were done from left to right, so that the meaning of a program like

```
1Ø PRINT 4−3+7
2Ø END
```

is obvious to the programmer and the computer.

The symbols + and − also have a meaning if they precede a number, for example in

```
1Ø PRINT −3
2Ø END
```

Used in this way, they give a sign to a value. This is not true of any other arithmetic symbol.

Exercise   Ensure that addition and subtraction and their combination is understood, by trying some programs.

3 Multiplication and division

Multiplication in BASIC is indicated by the symbol * written between the numbers to be multiplied. Like addition, it is of course order-independent, i.e. 5*3 is the same as 3*5.

Exercise   Try this:

```
1Ø PRINT 4.2*3.7
2Ø END
```

Here there are constants which have decimal points in them. This is always acceptable in BASIC.

In BASIC division occurs when the symbol / is used. Division is order-dependent so that

```
    6/3  is 2
and
    3/6  is 0.5
```

Exercise   Try some divisions. What does BASIC do about decimal points when the result of an integer division is not an integer? What if it is?

Exercise   Now mix multiplication with division. Do not include addition or subtraction yet.

4 Exponentiation

There is one more operation of arithmetic in BASIC, which is the raising of a number to a power. The keyboard symbol that should be used for this is ∧, because it resembles a vertical arrow. Sometimes, however, an actual vertical arrow is used. This is another order-dependent operation, so that

5$\wedge$3   means 125
and
3$\wedge$5   means 243

It is worth noting that fractional powers have their usual meaning:

2$\wedge$0.5   means $\sqrt{2}$ which is 1.4142 . . .

Any number raised to the power 0 gives the result 1, including 0$\wedge$0. It is wrong to raise 0 to a negative power, or to raise a negative number to a power which is not an integer.

Exercise   Try out exponentiation, still without mixing in other operations.

5 Expressions

The introduction of more general expressions has been delayed because there is a potential ambiguity in their meaning. For example, does

3+4*5   mean   (3+4)*5   which is 35
or   3+(4*5)   which is 23 ?

It may come as a surprise that the correct result is 23, in apparent contradiction to the statement that expressions give results as if they were evaluated from left to right. This is explained in the next section.

6 Rules of arithmetic in BASIC

In BASIC the rules of arithmetic are expressed in terms of a hierarchy of operations in which operations of high priority are performed before those of lower priority. The order is:

( )	quantities in brackets	high
$\wedge$	exponentiation	
* /	multiplication and division	
+ −	addition and subtraction	low

Hence in the expression 3+4*5, multiplication has a higher priority than addition so the meaning is 3+(4*5). Where priorities are equal, the result is like an evaluation from left to right. No two operators may appear in sequence so that 1+−2 is not allowed, although 1+(−2) is permitted because any self-contained expression can be preceded by a + or −. Therefore −3 is a meaningful expression on its own but *3 is not.

In BASIC the operation of multiplication must always be stated with the symbol *, i.e. as 3*4. The expression (3)(4) which in normal mathematical notation implies multiplication is incorrect in BASIC.

The availability of brackets provides a convenient means of changing or specifying the meaning of an expression because expressions within brackets are evaluated before the bracketed quantity is itself used.

Example   On a planet where the acceleration due to gravity is 3.11 metres per second per second and there is no atmosphere, a feather dropped from our spaceship hits the ground after 7.72 seconds. How high was the feather dropping platform? The formula is:

$$distance = \tfrac{1}{2} * acceleration * time^2$$

In this BASIC program which gives the answer, the only number to be squared is 7.72:

```
10 PRINT 0.5*3.11*7.72∧2
20 END
```

Exercise   Experiment with the meaning of the following and other expressions using BASIC. Clarify them with brackets, and change their meaning.

    4+5 /7   7/4*2/5   3/4/5   3∧4∧5   1+2∧3*4/5+6

7 Problems

Problem 2.1   Classify as true or false:

(i)	3*4∧2	is 144	(vii)	7/3+4	is 1
(ii)	3+4∧2	is 19	(viii)	4+5*3	is 19
(iii)	2+4/2	is 3	(ix)	3∧2*2	is 18
(iv)	2∧3+4	is 128	(x)	3/6/2	is 1
(v)	2∧2∧3	is 128	(xi)	2∧3∧2	is 64
(vi)	3*4+5	is 27	(xii)	9/3+2	is 5

Problem 2.2   State whether the meaning changes if the brackets are removed:

(i)	(3*4)∧5		(v)	2∧(3+4)
(ii)	(3∧4)*5		(vi)	2+(3∧4)
(iii)	2+(3*6)		(vii)	(2∧3)+4
(iv)	2*(3+6)		(viii)	(2+3)∧4

Problem 2.3   A racing driver completes 63.41 miles in 17 minutes 14.679 seconds. Doing all the calculations in BASIC, find the average speed.

Problem 2.4   Freddie deposited $1 in the Incredible Trust Company 9 years and one day ago. At the end of each month the Incredible has credited him with 0.62% interest. How much has he now?

UNIT 3

Communicating with BASIC

1 Introduction

It is now possible to show how communication with a BASIC program is arranged when it is running. The PRINT statement has already been encountered, and here facilities for printing messages as well as results are introduced. The usefulness of BASIC then takes a great leap forward with a method of providing values to running programs through the use of variables and the INPUT statement.

2 Printing captions—more about the PRINT statement

In a complicated program, interpretation of a stream of numbers printed by a running program can be very confusing unless explanatory messages are used in the presentation of results. In a PRINT statement messages or 'strings of characters' can be printed simply by enclosing them in quotation marks. BASIC then knows that what is enclosed by quotes is to be printed exactly as it appears.

As an example, consider again the sample program of Unit 1:

```
1Ø PRINT 2+2
2Ø END
```

which produced the numeric result 4. The line

```
1Ø PRINT "2+2"
```

will give a quite different result. Try it.

Exercise Try the program

```
1Ø PRINT "2+2 = "; 2+2
2Ø END
```

Several expressions to be printed must be separated by punctuation marks. A comma can be used, as in the example

```
1Ø PRINT 1,2+2,4+5/7,6.13*7.2
```

which arranges the output into columns of some fixed width. A semicolon is more useful because it squeezes values together:

```
1Ø  PRINT 1;2;3
```

Messages are usually in plain language, as in the following example which has two PRINT statements. Note that when this is run, each PRINT statement starts a new line.

```
1Ø  PRINT "THIS PROGRAM EVALUATES 2+2"
2Ø  PRINT "THE ANSWER IS "; 2+2
3Ø  END
```

To separate a message from a number which follows it, end the message with a space to make the output easier to read. It is not always necessary to do this when a message follows a number.

Exercise   Invent some programs with (polite) messages in them.

3   Dealing with large numbers

Some numbers are too large or too small to be printed conveniently in the normal way, and so an 'exponential format' used by PRINT statements and by programmers has been devised. The number is represented by a convenient number multiplied by a power of 10. For example,

The speed of light is 30 000 000 000 centimetres per second.
Scientists often write this as $3\text{x}10^{10}$ cm per second.
BASIC might write this as 3.0E10 or 3E10, where E means 'exponent'
Similarly $2.4\text{E}-23$ means $2.4\text{x}10^{-23}$
$$\text{or } 0.000\ 000\ 000\ 000\ 000\ 000\ 000\ 024$$

The exponential form is

$$n1\,\text{E}n2$$

where $n1$ and $n2$ are numbers and E is the letter E. This is interpreted as

$$n1\text{x}10^{n2}$$

It will be found that numbers which are too long to fit into convenient spaces will always be rendered by a PRINT statement into this form.

Exercise   Try the program

```
1Ø  PRINT "A BIG ONE IS "; 1ØØØ/.ØØØ1
2Ø  PRINT "AND A SMALL ONE "; .ØØØ1/1ØØØ
3Ø  END
```

A programmer might also wish to write large numbers compactly, and this can be done by writing constants in exponential form. The number 540,000 could be written in BASIC in several ways, for example

540000	as an integer
540000.0	with a decimal point
5.4E5	decimal point and exponent
54E4	integer and exponent

4 Inserting remarks—the REM statement

Documentation or 'writing up' is an important part of the job of programming, and making a program legible is a part of documenting it. Remarks or comments can be put in the written program which are intended to explain the program but which are not part of the printed output when it is run. The REM (for REMark) statement allows this. It is always good style to use them and they are essential in complicated programs.

The REM statement has the form

line number REM *any remark or comment*

and added to the sample program could be

```
1Ø REM A PROGRAM TO DEMONSTRATE BASIC
2Ø PRINT "THIS PROGRAM EVALUATES 2+2"
3Ø PRINT "THE ANSWER IS "; 2+2
4Ø END
```

5 Providing data to running programs—the INPUT statement

If a calculation is to be repeated several times with different numbers, it is inconvenient to spell out the constants each time by rewriting the program. Instead all programming languages allow the actual numbers to be entered when the program is run. In BASIC the INPUT statement does this. The program is written using symbolic names, much as in algebra, and an INPUT statement requests their values. Here is an example showing the INPUT statement and how variables are used instead of numbers.

```
1Ø INPUT A,B
2Ø PRINT (A+B)/2
3Ø END
```

At line 10, the program will request values for A and B. This request is indicated by a prompt from the computer; often a '?' is printed when it is ready. The programmer has commanded the program to RUN and waits for the '?' to appear. The numbers A and B are then entered with a comma between and a 'RETURN' at the end. After this the computer continues with the program—in this case to calculate the arithmetic mean $(A+B)/2$.

Actually the example is in poor style. The same computation in a better form is shown with its flowchart in Fig. 3.1. The features added to the program demonstrate four points of good style:

(i) REM statements are used to explain the purpose of the program.
(ii) Before INPUT is requested an explanatory message is issued at line 30.
(iii) The values of A and B are confirmed by the program at line 60.
(iv) The result is printed with an explanation at line 70.

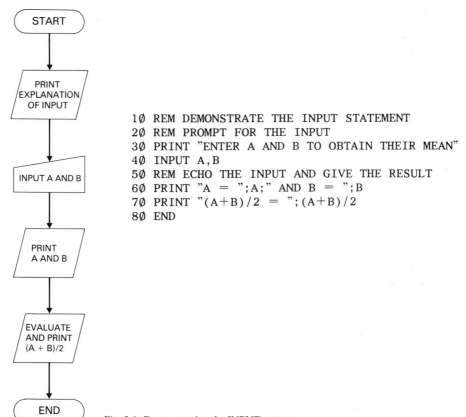

```
1Ø  REM DEMONSTRATE THE INPUT STATEMENT
2Ø  REM PROMPT FOR THE INPUT
3Ø  PRINT "ENTER A AND B TO OBTAIN THEIR MEAN"
4Ø  INPUT A,B
5Ø  REM ECHO THE INPUT AND GIVE THE RESULT
6Ø  PRINT "A = ";A;" AND B = ";B
7Ø  PRINT "(A+B)/2 = ";(A+B)/2
8Ø  END
```

Fig. 3.1. Demonstrating the INPUT statement

Exactly two numbers are expected by the INPUT statement at line 40. When the program is run and the '?' appears on the screen or terminal, exactly two numbers should be typed in with a comma between. If the wrong number of values is entered, a self-explanatory message will be issued. The numbers can be in exponential form.

Exercise Run the example, typing different values of A and B. Experiment with different expressions using more and fewer variables. Make deliberate errors in entering values, by entering too many or too few values. Finally, try some numbers in exponential form.

6   BASIC variables

In the previous section variables A and B were used in an example. There are 286 variable names allowed by BASIC. These are the single letters A to Z and the combination of any single letter followed by any single number, such as A0, A1, . . . A9, B0, B1, . . . B9, and so on.

Note that the letter O (oh) and the number 0 (zero) are easily confused. It is usually obvious what is intended, but when the wrong one has been used in error it can be difficult to spot. A widespread practice, adopted here for the programming examples, is to cross the number 0 (zero).

7   Assignment of values to variables—the LET statement

To begin with, in Unit 1, arithmetic was restricted to constants in PRINT statements. Then in this Unit it has been shown how variables could be used instead, but up to this point their values could only be assigned by manual entry using INPUT statements. Now it will be seen that assignments can be made using a special statement, the LET statement.

The following is an example:

        2Ø LET B=3

which assigns the value 3 to the variable B. Until statement 20 it is likely that B was not defined and so could not be used in expressions. This is because a variable has no value until one is assigned—although some computers give initial values of zero. To write programs that can be moved from one computer to another, never assume that a variable is given an initial value. As soon as line 20 is complete the value of B is definitely 3. More complicated expressions often occur, such as

        73 LET D=B∧2−4*A*C

which looks like the calculation of the discriminant b^2-4ac of the quadratic equation $ax^2+bx+c=0$. A, B and C must be known before line 73 is reached, otherwise the computer will object. If they are known the expression of the right hand side is evaluated and the result is assigned as the new value of variable D.

The general form of a LET statement is

line number LET *variable* = *expression*

When a LET statement is encountered, the *expression* on the right hand side is evaluated. The result replaces the value of the *variable* on the left hand side. The effect is therefore assignment of a value to the *variable*. LET statements are commonly called 'assignment statements' or 'replacement statements'. Although some computers will allow the keyword LET to be left out of assignment statements, it is very poor practice to take advantage of this. If the word LET is always used, then the program will not fail on other computers, at least not for that particular reason!

Example Suppose a program is converting feet and inches to metres. The number of inches in a metre is a constant, 39.3701, and so a constant is used. The data is requested through an INPUT statement and then converted to inches using a LET statement. The value in metres is then calculated with a LET statement, and one PRINT statement produces the data in inches, along with the metric equivalent. The use of LET statements has simplified the PRINT statement, avoided repetitions of the same calculation which would be needed to print all the results on one line, and made the program easy to follow. The program and flowchart are shown in Fig. 3.2.

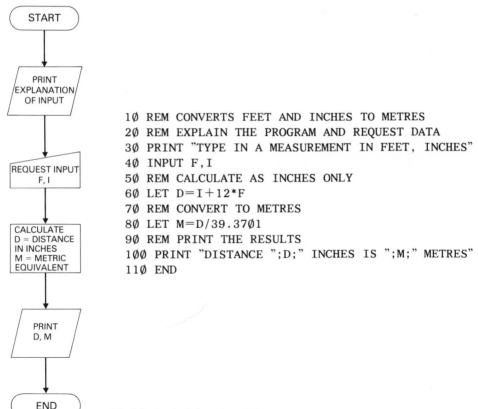

```
10  REM CONVERTS FEET AND INCHES TO METRES
20  REM EXPLAIN THE PROGRAM AND REQUEST DATA
30  PRINT "TYPE IN A MEASUREMENT IN FEET, INCHES"
40  INPUT F,I
50  REM CALCULATE AS INCHES ONLY
60  LET D=I+12*F
70  REM CONVERT TO METRES
80  LET M=D/39.3701
90  REM PRINT THE RESULTS
100 PRINT "DISTANCE ";D;" INCHES IS ";M;" METRES"
110 END
```

Fig. 3.2. A calculation using LET statements

Example   In many countries, a tax is added to the price of goods at the point of sale. This little program adds tax at 15% to a price:

```
10 REM ADDS 15% TAX TO A SALE PRICE
20 PRINT "ENTER THE PRICE BEFORE TAX AT 15%"
30 INPUT PØ
40 LET P1=PØ*1.15
50 PRINT PØ;" BEFORE TAX BECOMES ";P1;" AFTER."
60 END
```

and this one takes it away. If the price is \$1.00 after tax, it isn't \$0.85 before tax, although it is a very common mistake to think so. Try it and see!

```
10 REM REMOVES 15% TAX FROM A PRICE
20 PRINT "ENTER THE PRICE AFTER TAX AT 15%"
30 INPUT P1
40 LET PØ=P1/1.15
50 PRINT P1;" AFTER TAX WAS ";PØ;" BEFORE."
60 END
```

8   Problems

However simple a problem may seem, it is always worthwhile to prepare a flowchart and write the solution out by hand before attempting it on the computer. It is good style to give messages which explain the nature and layout of input data before it is requested, and printed output should be accompanied by explanations too.

Problem 3.1   Write a program to square a number which is typed in. Using this program search for the square root of 63 to three significant figures, by running the program as many times as are necessary.

Problem 3.2   Write a program which calculates the return r on compound interest:

$$r = (1 + i/100)^n$$

where $i =$ interest in percent and $n =$ number of periods, or number of times the interest has been compounded.

Using this program, RUN it several times and search for the integer number of periods n taken to at least double an investment at $i = 4\%$, 6% and 8%.

Problem 3.3   Write a program to convert the time of day on a 24 hour clock given as hours minutes and seconds to a decimal time system, in which for example 18:30:00 is 18.50 hours.

UNIT 4

Repeating calculations

1 Introduction

Many applications of programming in both the business and scientific world require programs to be repeated over and over, perhaps with new data as in payroll accounts, or perhaps with some variable changing in a regular way. Several ways of organising and controlling this kind of repetition will be found in Units which follow, but here the simplest case is introduced and then applied to some quite sophisticated calculations.

2 Repeating calculations—the GO TO statement

The GO TO statement enables a programmer to change the order in which the statements of a program are obeyed. When a GO TO is encountered, the program jumps to a new place as specified in the GO TO statement. It has the form

this line number GO TO *another line number*

This *line number* is just the line number of the statement itself, but *another line number* is another statement of the program which is the target for the jump. For example,

    5Ø GO TO 1Ø

causes the computer to jump to line 10 rather than carrying on to the next line number after 50. The BASIC standard requires GO TO to have a space in it between GO and TO, but many implementations break this rule and insist on GOTO as one word.

Once a program has been organised to repeat itself, it could go on endlessly unless some way has been arranged to stop it. One of the simplest ways is available if the repetition contains an INPUT statement as in Fig. 4.1. In this case, when the program requests data, the programmer can usually type in STOP.

If a program loop is printing continuously, it can be stopped from the keyboard. Programming accidents do occur from time to time so every BASIC user should know how to interrupt a program; the method of doing this varies between systems. Often the BREAK or ESCAPE keys are used.

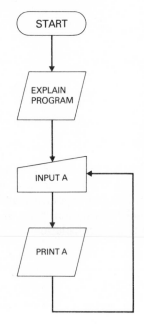

```
1Ø REM PROGRAM TO DEMONSTRATE ENDLESS REPETITION
2Ø PRINT "THIS PROGRAM ASKS FOR ONE INPUT VALUE"
3Ø PRINT "IT REPEATS UNTIL YOU STOP IT"
4Ø INPUT A
5Ø REM PRINT IT AND RETURN FOR MORE
6Ø PRINT "YOU TYPED IN ";A;" HOW ABOUT SOME MORE"
7Ø GO TO 4Ø
8Ø END
```

Fig. 4.1. A program repeated by a GO TO statement

Exercise　Find out from an expert how to interrupt a program on your computer. Run and terminate the following example:

```
1Ø REM A PAPER EATING PROGRAM
2Ø PRINT "STOP ME"
3Ø GO TO 2Ø
4Ø END
```

3　Self-replacement in LET statements

It is interesting to enquire what will happen if the same variable is used on both sides in a LET statement, such as

```
99 LET J=J+1
```

The simple answer is that J has been used in calculating its own replacement value. This statement is one of self-replacement and one of its important uses is in counting. A program which counts by ones from 1 is shown in Fig. 4.2, which illustrates an important kind of loop. This is another program requiring manual intervention.

Exercise　Try the program of Fig. 4.2.

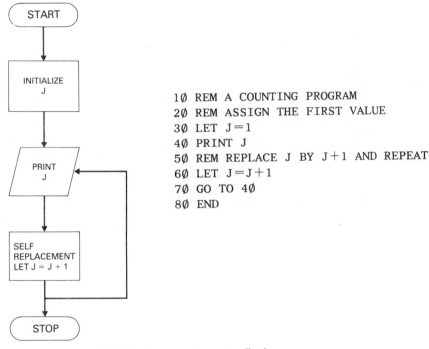

```
10 REM A COUNTING PROGRAM
20 REM ASSIGN THE FIRST VALUE
30 LET J=1
40 PRINT J
50 REM REPLACE J BY J+1 AND REPEAT
60 LET J=J+1
70 GO TO 40
80 END
```

Fig. 4.2. A program to count endlessly

There is no reason why the self-replacement cannot be of a more complicated type. Here is a program which forms successive squares of a number typed in.

```
10 REM FORM SUCCESSIVE SQUARES OF A NUMBER
20 PRINT "ENTER NUMBER FOR SUCCESSIVE SQUARING"
30 INPUT A
40 PRINT A;" SQUARED IS ";A*A
50 LET A=A*A
60 GO TO 40
70 END
```

4   Real programming—recurrence

By looking at self-replacement in more complicated cases than simple counting, it can be seen that a number of useful types of calculation can be undertaken. First of all, it is often useful to be able to add things up. To do this a variable is used to hold the sum, which is initialised before the loop, and new additions are made each time around the loop. It is inconvenient at this stage that the loop cannot be stopped automatically, but this problem will be cleared up in the next Unit.

Figure 4.3 shows a program that counts from 1 by ones and adds up the total counts at the same time to find $1+2+3\ldots$. It is similar in structure to Fig. 4.2 but with the sum built in.

Exercise   Run the program of Fig. 4.3. Recall that it must be stopped manually. If the formula for the sum of an arithmetic progression is known, check the results.

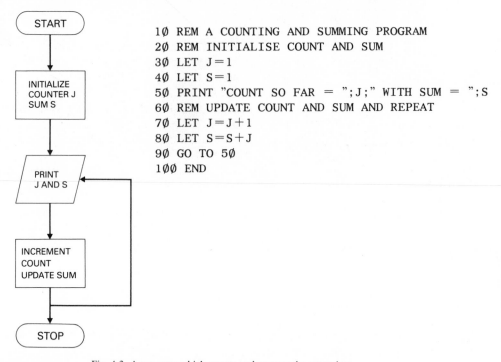

```
1Ø REM A COUNTING AND SUMMING PROGRAM
2Ø REM INITIALISE COUNT AND SUM
3Ø LET J=1
4Ø LET S=1
5Ø PRINT "COUNT SO FAR = ";J;" WITH SUM = ";S
6Ø REM UPDATE COUNT AND SUM AND REPEAT
7Ø LET J=J+1
8Ø LET S=S+J
9Ø GO TO 5Ø
1ØØ END
```

Fig. 4.3. A program which counts and sums at the same time

One important use of this kind of loop is called recurrence. This arises when a sum of complicated terms is being found, but the clever programmer can see some relationship between the terms, which makes the calculation more efficient. For example suppose the sum is

$$1+x+x^2+\ldots$$

A clever programmer would realise that raising a number to a power is expensive in terms of computer time and that each new term is just the previous one multiplied by x. In the program at line 120 the new term is calculated as follows:

```
1Ø REM SUM POWERS OF X
2Ø PRINT "TYPE IN A NUMBER TO SUM ITS POWERS"
3Ø INPUT X
4Ø REM INITIALISE COUNT J, TERM T, AND SUM S
5Ø LET S=Ø
6Ø LET T=1
7Ø LET J=1
```

```
80 REM ADD ON LATEST TERM
90 LET S=S+T
100 PRINT "TERM ";J;" IS ";T;" SUM IS ";S
110 REM MOVE TO NEXT TERM
120 LET J=J+1
130 LET T=T*X
140 GO TO 90
150 END
```

Example This is a famous sum. If you walk one mile today, half a mile tomorrow, and then each day half as far as the previous day, do you ever get to a destination which is two miles away? This little program uses recurrence to compute the new distance travelled each day, and the total covered so far:

```
10 REM DO THE SUM 1 + 1/2 + 1/4 + ...
20 LET D=1
30 LET M=1
40 LET S=0
50 PRINT "TODAY IS DAY ";D;" AND YOU WALKED ";M;" MILES."
60 LET S=S+M
70 PRINT "YOUR JOURNEY SO FAR IS ";S;" MILES IN TOTAL."
80 LET D=D+1
90 LET M=M/2
100 GO TO 50
110 END
```

Exercise For x between -1 and 1 the series $1+x+x^2+ \ldots$ taken to many terms eventually becomes the same as $1/(1-x)$. Try the program and check the result. What happens if x is 1? What happens if x is close to 1?

5 Problems

Problem 4.1 Write a program which prints successive powers of 2 in an endless loop. It will have to be stopped manually.

Problem 4.2 Your computer will have a limit to the size of numbers it can cope with. Find this limit roughly by successive squaring of 10 (10, 10^2, 10^4, 10^8, etc.) and then try to locate it more accurately. You may be surprised at how large it is.

Problem 4.3 Write a program which adds up numbers you enter at the keyboard and counts them as well. Each time round print the count, the sum, and the average so far.

Problem 4.4 The Maclaurin series for e^x is

$$e^x = 1 + x + x^2/2 + x^3/3! + x^4/4! + \ldots$$

Discover a recurrence relationship between the terms and write a program to make the sum in an endless loop.

UNIT 5
Making decisions

1   Introduction

A powerful and fundamental facility of all computer languages is the ability to compare or test quantities in order to decide the course of the calculation. In other words, a kind of GO TO can be arranged to happen only when certain conditions are satisfied. This is probably the most important single advance to be made in any Unit and it is worth considerable effort. Using the material presented to the end of this Unit, most applications of computing are possible. The Units which follow may introduce facilities of great convenience, but the foundations are laid in the first five Units.

2   Relational expressions

So far the expressions encountered in BASIC have been those of simple arithmetic, involving the operations $+$, $-$, $*$, $/$, and $\wedge$. A different kind of expression is the relational expression which is used to make comparisons between quantities or expressions. In BASIC a relational expression decides whether a relationship between two quantities is TRUE or FALSE.

For example the relational expression

    A>1Ø*B

will be TRUE if A is greater than 10*B, otherwise it is FALSE. TRUE and FALSE are the only possible results of a relational expression.

The general form of a relational expression is

   arithmetic   relational   arithmetic
   expression   operator   expression

Therefore any two arithmetic expressions can be compared. The available relational operators are

$=$	equal to	$>=$	greater or equal
$>$	greater than	$<=$	less or equal
$<$	less than	$<>$	not equal

Examples

1Ø $>$1Ø	is FALSE	B$\wedge$2$-$4*A*C $<$Ø	only one of these
1Ø $=$1Ø	is TRUE	B$\wedge$2$-$4*A*C $=$Ø	can be TRUE.
5 $<=$6	is TRUE	B$\wedge$2$-$4*A*C $>$Ø	
A $=$B	is TRUE	if A equals B, otherwise FALSE	

3   Decisions—the IF ... THEN statement

The IF . . . THEN statement uses a relational expression to make a decision about whether or not to jump to a chosen line number. This allows programs to determine their own course of events based on conditions that arise when running. The form of the IF . . . THEN statement is

line number a IF *relational expression* THEN *line number b*

Here *line number a* is the line number of the statement itself. When the computer encounters it a decision is made about which line to execute next. If the *relational expression* is TRUE, the computer jumps to *line number b* as if a GO TO had sent it there. If the *relational expression* is FALSE, then the next line in sequence after *line number a* is executed next in the normal way.

Example

```
2Ø IF I=1Ø THEN 5Ø
3Ø
4Ø
5Ø
```

In this example, when execution reaches line 20, the value of I is compared to 10. If I$=$10 then the program jumps to line 50. Otherwise it continues in the usual way with line 30. Therefore a way of skipping directly to line 50 has been provided if I$=$10 at line 20.

Example   The counting program which was presented in Fig. 4.2 can be made to stop after the fifth term by replacing line 70 with

```
7Ø IF J<=5 THEN 4Ø
```

which produces the program shown in Fig. 5.1.

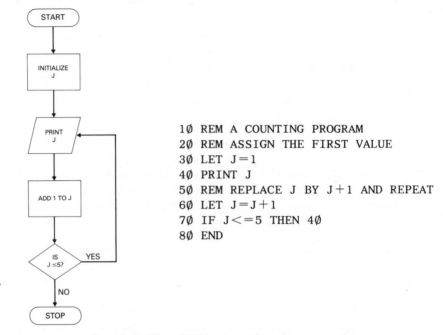

10 REM A COUNTING PROGRAM
20 REM ASSIGN THE FIRST VALUE
30 LET J=1
40 PRINT J
50 REM REPLACE J BY J+1 AND REPEAT
60 LET J=J+1
70 IF J<=5 THEN 40
80 END

Fig. 5.1. An IF . . . THEN statement is used to stop counting

In introducing the IF . . . THEN facility it is necessary to make a few remarks about program style. Armed with this decision maker it is possible to create very involved programs, but it is poor style to have a more compex structure than is necessary. Good programs generally read from the top down without involved jumps back and forth. One fault shared by many inexperienced users is a tendency to follow an IF . . . THEN immediately by an unnecessary GO TO. Looking again at the counting program, Fig. 4.2, the change could have been made to have a new line 65:

    65 IF J>5 THEN 80
    70 GO TO 40

This is terrible style as can be seen by considering how this would complicate the flowchart of Fig. 5.1.

While standards of documentation may vary considerably, flowcharts are often used. They are used by many programmers in the design of programs of any complexity, and the finished programs are sometimes documented by a complete flowchart. Figure 5.2 shows the meaning of the various flowchart shapes used in this text.

Example   Here is a program which takes three numbers A, B and C and arranges them in order so that A≤B≤C. Do you see the purpose of the temporary variable T?

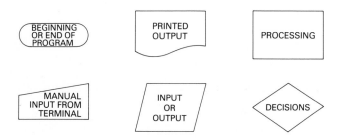

Fig. 5.2. Conventional symbols for flowcharts.

```
10 REM PLACE A, B, C IN ORDER
20 PRINT "ENTER THREE VALUES TO BE ORDERED"
30 INPUT A,B,C
40 REM REORDER A AND B IF REQUIRED
50 IF B>A THEN 110
60 REM SWITCH A AND B
70 LET T=A
80 LET A=B
90 LET B=T
100 REM DOES C GO BEFORE A?
110 IF C>A THEN 190
120 REM PUT C BEFORE A
130 LET T=C
140 LET C=B
150 LET B=A
160 LET A=T
170 GO TO 250
180 REM OTHERWISE DOES C GO BEFORE B?
190 IF C>B THEN 250
200 REM PUT C BEFORE B
210 LET T=C
220 LET C=B
230 LET B=T
240 REM ALL FINISHED, SHOW THEM OFF
250 PRINT "HERE THEY ARE IN ORDER ";A;B;C
260 END
```

Exercise The program just given to order A, B and C is called an insertion sort, because it inserts first B and then C in the correct place. Make a flowchart of it. Can you think of other ways of placing three values in order, and make BASIC programs to do it? Try for a method whose flowchart is as straightforward as possible.

4   A real problem—Newton's method

It is now possible to attempt some more interesting calculations. Because of the decision making feature these programs will be more complex than before. In this section, the procedures involved in designing and implementing a fairly typical numerical problem are gone over in some detail.

The problem to be considered is the Newton—Raphson method for solving an equation such as

$$f(x) = 0$$

to find values of x which satisfy the equation. The method is based on the simple notion that if a guess is made at the answer, the slope of the function can be used to find a better answer by pretending the function is a straight line.

In Fig. 5.3, at $x = g$ (for guess) f is the function value and p is the slope. Then a better guess will be at b where it can be shown that

$$b = g - f/p$$

All that is needed is an equation for $f(x)$ and its slope p.

Consider the specific problem now of finding the square root of 2. The function $f(x)$ becomes

$$x^2 - 2 = 0$$

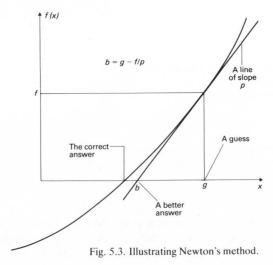

Fig. 5.3. Illustrating Newton's method.

which has the solution $\sqrt{2}$. The slope of this function is $2x$. Therefore, to find $\sqrt{2}$, a guess g is made, and the slope is calculated at g. A better guess b is then calculated from it. Then we do this again, using b as the guess so that a further improved approximation to the root can be calculated. We use the same statements each time around to give better and better values of b—and this is another example of recurrence.

To implement this method, first a flowchart is drawn to make sure that the procedure is understood. The flowchart for this example is shown in Fig. 5.4. Particular notice should be taken of the replacement of g by b in the return path. This causes each improved estimate to be used again so that further improvements are obtained automatically. As a matter of good practice, it should be noted that the programmer has decided to print the results of every calculation in the procedure. This is always worthwhile because new programs are almost certain to contain mistakes. A liberal spread of PRINT statements throughout a calculation is always useful. To find mistakes in a program it is essential to be able to locate where trouble first appears, and this can only be done with a generous amount of information.

In order to translate Fig. 5.4 into BASIC, suitable variable names are chosen, in this case

F to represent $f(x)$ G to represent g, the guess
P to represent p, the slope   B to represent b, the better guess

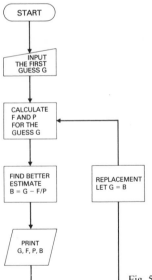

Fig. 5.4. Flowchart of Newton's method.

By referring to the flowchart, the program can be written out in skeleton form and checked carefully before it is typed in at the keyboard and tried. The following is a possible solution:

```
1Ø PRINT "TYPE IN A GUESS AT SQR(2)"
2Ø INPUT G
3Ø LET F=G*G−2
4Ø LET P=2*G
5Ø LET B=G−F/P
6Ø PRINT "AT ";G;" F IS ";F;" SLOPE ";P;" NEW GUESS ";B
7Ø LET G=B
8Ø GO TO 3Ø
9Ø END
```

The next stage is to dress the program up with REM statements so that it can be understood if it is looked at by someone else, or indeed by the original programmer after the passage of time. This example is considerably improved by the addition of remarks:

```
1Ø CALCULATION OF SQR(2) BY NEWTON'S METHOD
2Ø REM BY SOLVING X∧2−2=Ø
3Ø REM FIRST ACCEPT AN ESTIMATE OF THE ANSWER
4Ø PRINT "TYPE IN AN ESTIMATE OF SQR(2)"
5Ø INPUT G
6Ø REM CALCULATE FUNCTION VALUE F AND SLOPE P
7Ø LET F=G*G−2
8Ø LET P=2*G
9Ø REM NOW CALCULATE AN IMPROVED GUESS B
1ØØ LET B=G−F/P
11Ø PRINT "AT ";G;" F IS ";F;" SLOPE ";P;" NEW GUESS ";B
12Ø REM USE B AS THE ESTIMATE NEXT TIME ROUND
13Ø LET G=B
14Ø GO TO 7Ø
15Ø END
```

Exercise   Try this program. As yet it has no IF . . .THEN statements. Now improve it in two ways. First of all, after line 40 check that the estimate is between 0 and 2—otherwise the guess is silly. Secondly before line 130 calculate how different B is from G, and stop if the difference is less than 0.000 01. The square root of 2 is 1.414 . . . . Does this program work? Draw a flowchart of it.

5   Another decider—the ON . . . GO TO statement

It is sometimes useful to be able to jump to one of several destinations in a program. The ON . . . GO TO statement arranges this although it is used much less often than IF . . . THEN. Its form is *line number ON expression GO TO line no a, line no b, . . .*

When this statement is reached, the *expression* is worked out. Then if the integer part of the result is 1, the program jumps to *line no a*, if 2 it jumps to *line no b*, and so on for however many destinations are given. If the *expression* turns out to be negative, zero, or larger than the number of destinations given, then an error has been made and a suitable message will appear on the screen.

Example

```
5Ø  ON  SGN(B∧2−4*A*C)+2  GO  TO  1ØØ,2ØØ,3ØØ
```

A statement like this would be used in solving Problem 5.3. The SGN function, which is introduced in the next chapter, gives -1 if the expression in brackets is negative, 0 if it is 0 and 1 if positive. Therefore adding 2 to it gives 1, 2 or 3 for the ON . . . GO TO.

6 Problems

Problem 5.1   Write a program which prints successive powers of 2 and stops after 2^{10}.

Problem 5.2   Rewrite the program for Newton's method to find the square root of any number. Only accept guesses between 0 and the number whose square root is sought. Stop the calculation with an IF . . . THEN statement when the the answer ceases to change appreciably.

Problem 5.3   Write a program to find the roots of a quadratic equation $ax^2+bx+c=0$ where *a*, *b*, and *c* are given as input from the keyboard. Use an ON . . . GO TO statement to separate the three possible conditions that will arise in the discriminant. This will require some thought.

Problem 5.4   Write a program to find the root of an equation $ax^3+bx^2+cx+d=0$ where *a*, *b*, *c*, and *d* are given as input from the keyboard, using Newton's method. Ask for help with the expression for slope if necessary. Find one of the roots of the polynomial $x^3-7.8x^2+18.5x-11.3=0$ using this program. Does it work for any guess? Draw the function to see why—use BASIC to tabulate values of the function.

UNIT 6
Built-in functions

1 Introduction

Certain calculations tend to occur over and over again in BASIC programs, and many of these use the values of common functions which are not easy to compute. The calculation of a square root is a good example of this; it is inconvenient to write out a long program to do a square root every time one is needed. Like all computer languages, BASIC has built in 'library' functions which evaluate often-used functions. To find a square root the SQR function is used.

2 Library functions in BASIC

The list of functions available in BASIC varies considerably between systems. All versions should include the following mathematical ones:

Function	Meaning
SQR(*expression*)	Square root of *expression*
ABS(*expression*)	Absolute value of *expression*
SGN(*expression*)	Sign of *expression*: 1 if > 0, 0 if 0, -1 if < 0
INT(*expression*)	Largest integer not greater than *expression*
EXP(*expression*)	The value of $e^{expression}$
LOG(*expression*)	Natural logarithm (base e) of *expression*
SIN(*expression*)	Sine of *expression*, *expression* in radians
COS(*expression*)	Cosine of *expression*, *expression* in radians
TAN(*expression*)	Tangent of *expression*, *expression* in radians
ATN(*expression*)	The angle in the range $-\pi/2$ to $\pi/2$ radians whose tangent is *expression*

The function RND, which is a random number generator, also appears in most versions of BASIC, together with the RANDOMIZE function.

To use a function, simply write it into any expression where it is desired with its 'argument' in brackets immediately after it. For example:

```
2Ø PRINT SQR(2)
```

prints the square root of 2.

3 Trying them out

Here the functions given in the previous section are considered individually, except for INT which is looked at in detail later.

(a) SQR

The square root function saves programmers the trouble of devising a numerical method for finding square roots every time they need one. The only thing to remember when using it is that a negative number does not have a real square root. The following program uses SQR to find the hypotenuse of a right-angled triangle, given the other two sides:

```
1Ø  PRINT "THIS PROGRAM FINDS THE HYPOTENUSE"
2Ø  PRINT "TYPE IN TWO SIDES"
3Ø  INPUT A,B
4Ø  PRINT "HYPOTENUSE= ";SQR(A*A+B*B)
5Ø  GO TO 2Ø
6Ø  END
```

Exercise   Try this example. It will give no trouble about negative arguments. Then find out what happens if SQR is given a negative argument.

(b) ABS

This function forces the sign of an expression to be positive. It can be used to keep out of trouble with SQR, as in

```
6ØØ  LET  T=SQR(ABS(X))
```

Very often a program is interested in the size of a value regardless of its sign, and this is when ABS is used. In some problems in Unit 7 the size of a term in a power series will be used to stop adding more terms.

(c) SGN

Sometimes it may be important to know when a number is positive or negative independently of the value. Problem 5.3 was difficult without the SGN function. To test the discriminant of a quadratic expression $Ax^2 + Bx + C$ an ON . . . GO TO statement can be used with

```
SGN(B*B−4*A*C)+2
```

which has the values 1, 2, or 3 for negative, zero, or positive values of the discriminant.

SGN can be used to transfer the sign of one variable to another. Suppose Z is to have the same magnitude as X but the same sign as Y. This can be achieved by combining the SGN and ABS functions as in

    9Ø LET Z=SGN(Y)*ABS(X)

which will work except when Y is zero.

(d) EXP and LOG

These two mathematical functions go together, and are based on e (2.718 281 828 45). EXP raises e to a power, and LOG finds the logarithm to the base e. Therefore if

$$Y = EXP(X) \quad \text{then} \quad X = LOG(Y)$$

The log function can easily be used to base 10 or any other base by recalling that

$$\log_a X = \log_e X \log_a e = \frac{\log_e X}{\log_e a}$$

so that the log of X to base 10 could be found using a statement like

    11Ø LET L=LOG(X)/LOG(1Ø)

or to base *a* by

    11Ø LET L=LOG(X)/LOG(A)

Exercise   Print the value of e.

(e) SIN, COS and TAN

These trigonometric functions of an angle, as illustrated in Fig. 6.1, are often used. In BASIC the angle is in radians and this may not always be convenient, although conversion is easy since π radians is the same as 180°. A simple way to calculate π is mentioned under the ATN function which follows.

Exercise   Check using the BASIC functions for a few angles that

   (i) $\sin^2 x + \cos^2 x = 1$ (ii) $\tan x = \sin x / \cos x$

(f) ATN

The ATN or arctangent function is one which can give conceptual difficulty. The argument of the function is the value of a tangent, and the result is the angle that goes with it. For example the tangent of 45° is 1. Therefore the function

    ATN(1)

gives the angle in radians whose tangent is 1, i.e. $\pi/4$ radians. This useful result can be used to convert degrees to radians and *vice versa*.

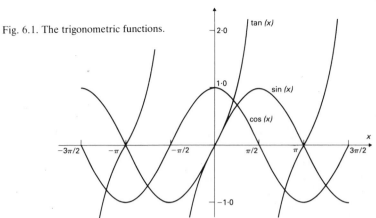

Fig. 6.1. The trigonometric functions.

Often the value of π is wanted. This can be derived by writing

    1ØØ LET P=4*ATN(1)

There is an ambiguity in the ATN function because if the tangent is x, then the angle could be A, say, but also $A\pm\pi/2$, $A\pm\pi$, and so on. This is why the ATN function gives an answer between $-\pi/2$ and $\pi/2$, which is an unambiguous range as can be seen in Fig. 6.1.

Using this information, it is easy to see that the following statement converts D in degrees to R in radians:

    2ØØ LET R=D*ATN(1)/45

and this converts R in radians to D in degrees:

    3ØØ LET D=R*45/ATN(1)

4   Truncation and its uses

Probably the most useful function of them all is the INT function. Precisely speaking, $\text{INT}(x)$ provides a value which is the largest integer which is not greater than x. Accordingly

    $\text{INT}(5.95)$ is 5   and $\text{INT}(-5.95)$ is -6

Look carefully at the second example.

(a) Rounding

Often it is necessary to round a result to the nearest whole number, or to a certain number of decimal places. Although INT does not do this directly, it is easily forced to do so. To round x to the nearest whole number, simply add 0.5 before using INT:

$$400 \text{ LET } Y = INT(X + 0.5)$$

A simple extension to this idea enables rounding to be taken to any scale. Scale the data so that the resolution desired is represented by successive integers, add 0.5, use INT and then reverse the scaling.

Examples

(i)   Round to two decimal places (to the nearest 0.01):

$$400 \text{ LET } Y = INT(X*100 + 0.5)/100$$

(ii) Round to the nearest 100:

$$400 \text{ LET } Y = INT(X/100 + 0.05)*100$$

(iii) Round to the nearest 4:

$$400 \text{ LET } Y = INT(X/4 + 0.05)*4$$

(b) Truncation

The term truncation applies to the removal of decimal places, and so the function INT as it stands is not quite a truncation because of its operation on negative numbers. However the expression

$$SGN(X)*INT(ABS(X))$$

does truncate X, as does INT itself for positive numbers.

Truncation is useful when the remainder after division is required. This happens when numbers are being converted from one base to another and when units are being converted. In dividing 22 by 7 the integer part of the quotient is 3 and the remainder is 1. If the quotient were N/D with N positive, then the integer part would be

$$INT(N/D)$$

and the remainder

$$N - INT(N/D)*D$$

However if N or D could be negative, the integer part would be

$$SGN(N/D)*INT(ABS(N/D))$$

and the unsigned remainder is

$$ABS(N) - INT(ABS(N/D))*ABS(D)$$

(c) Base conversion

To convert numbers between bases, the old number is divided by the new base over and over again with the remainders forming the number in the new base.

Example   131 decimal to base 7:

Step 1	$131/7 = 18$	remainder 5
Step 2	$18/7 = 2$	remainder 4
Step 3	$2/7 = 0$	remainder 2

The answer is 5 units, 4 sevens, and 2 forty-nines, i.e. 245 in base 7.

(d) Units conversion

There are many cases of units of measurement with mixed bases, particularly in the English system. For example a time measurement in days, hours, minutes and seconds is in bases 24, 60, and 60. To convert 18.43 days into hours, minutes, and seconds requires the following BASIC statements:

```
100 REM GET WHOLE HOURS
110 LET H=INT(24*18.43)
120 REM REMAINING PART HOUR
130 LET R=18.43*24-H
140 REM WHOLE MINUTES
150 LET M=INT(60*R)
160 REM REMAINING PART MINUTE
170 LET R=60*R-M
180 REM FINALLY SECONDS WITH DECIMAL PLACES
190 LET S=60*R
```

At the end the time is in variables H, M, and S.

5   Random numbers

The function RND looks up a number between 0 and 1 which is apparently random. It isn't actually random, it just appears to be. There are some variations in the way that RND has been implemented on different computers. This section follows the standard.

RND should be written without an argument. This little program will print ten apparently unrelated numbers:

```
1Ø REM GET SOME RANDOM NUMBERS        4Ø LET I=I+1
2Ø LET I=1                            5Ø IF I<11 THEN 3Ø
3Ø PRINT RND                          6Ø END
```

If it won't work, it is probably because the particular computer requires an argument. Try RND(0) if that is the case.

Running this RND program several times should produce the same numbers each time. If different numbers are required each time, put in the RANDOMIZE statement which tells RND to select an apparently random starting number. This program tosses a coin ten times:

```
1Ø REM TOSS A COIN
2Ø RANDOMIZE
3Ø LET I=1
4Ø LET C=RND
5Ø IF C<Ø.5 THEN 8Ø
6Ø PRINT "TAIL"              9Ø LET I=I+1
7Ø GO TO 9Ø                  1ØØ IF I<11 THEN 4Ø
8Ø PRINT "HEAD"              11Ø END
```

6   Problems

Problem 6.1   The period *T* seconds of a pendulum of length *l* metres for a small angle of swing is

$$T = 2\pi \sqrt{l/g}$$

where $g = 9.81$ metres per second per second, the acceleration due to gravity.

(a) Write a program to find the period from the length.
(b) Write a program to find the length from the period.

Check these programs against each other.

Problem 6.2   Given two sides adjacent to the right angle in a triangle, calculate the length of the hypotenuse and find the other two angles in degrees.

Problem 6.3   Write a program to convert a decimal number to any base from 2 to 9. Do this in a loop; it is acceptable that the results are produced in reverse order. Make it work for positive or negative numbers.

Problem 6.4   Write a program using RANDOMIZE and RND to throw two dice and report the sum of their spots.

UNIT 7
Program loops

1 Introduction

In many earlier problems and examples, programs were encountered which included repeated calculations or loops. It has been seen how an IF . . . THEN statement is used to control a loop. In many calculations the number of repetitions of a loop is known before the loop, and in these cases BASIC has a special facility for organising them.

2 Forming a loop

Many programs require calculations to be repeated a fixed number of times. Loops can be set up and controlled using a LET statement for initialisation and counting, and later on an IF . . . THEN statement to test for completion. Initialisation, counting, and testing are the common features of a counting loop.

Suppose a calculation is to be repeated 10 times. A variable I can be set aside to count the number of times the loop has been executed. Before the loop is entered, I is initialised by being set to one. Each time the end of the loop is reached, I is increased by one and then tested to see if the loop is complete. Figure 7.1 illustrates a typical flowchart for looping.

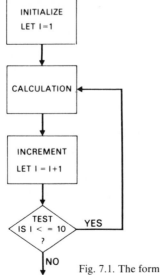

Fig. 7.1. The form of a counting loop.

3   The easy way—the FOR and NEXT statements

BASIC has two special statements to make loop formation easier for a programmer. The definition of the loop is accomplished by a FOR statement which gives all the information about the initial and final values of the counter and the step size in between. The NEXT statement identifies the end of the loop.

As an example, suppose a variable I is to be used to count 10 passes around a loop. The FOR and NEXT statements could be as follows:

```
7Ø FOR I=1 TO 1Ø

9Ø
1ØØ    (a calculation)
11Ø
13Ø NEXT I
```

The convenience of this is obvious. The general form of the FOR statement is

line number FOR *variable* = *expression* TO *expression* STEP *expression*

Example The FOR and NEXT statements often make summation very easy. This little program adds up the numbers from 1 to 12. It tells you how many gifts you receive on the twelfth day of Christmas according to the famous carol:

```
1Ø REM ADD THE NUMBERS FROM 1 TO 12
2Ø REM USE S FOR THE SUM AND G FOR THE GIFTS
3Ø LET S=Ø
4Ø FOR G=1 TO 12
5Ø LET S=S+G
6Ø NEXT G
7Ø PRINT "THE SUM OF THE INTEGERS FROM 1 TO 12 IS ";S
8Ø END
```

The meaning of the FOR statement should be quite clear although there are a number of rules of detail which the following points should clarify:

(i)   A variable name must be used as the index or loop counter. It does not have to be referred to in the calculation itself, as in this example using K as a counter:

```
1Ø FOR K=1 TO 5
2Ø PRINT "LOOP"
3Ø NEXT K
```

(ii)   The initial and final values are given in the FOR statement.

(iii) The STEP part is optional. If STEP is left out, the step size is 1. It can be fractional or negative, as in

```
1Ø FOR X=Ø.25 TO 1.5Ø STEP Ø.25
     .

     .

     .
8Ø NEXT X
```

and

```
2ØØ FOR P=1Ø TO 1 STEP −1
     .

     .

     .
53Ø NEXT P
```

(iv) The limits and the step size can be any expression.

(v) If the initial, final, and step values are such that the loop should not be executed, it is jumped over according to the BASIC standard. Unfortunately this rule is not always followed, and many versions of BASIC run through the loop once anyway. In standard BASIC the message in this short program should not be printed. Try yours and see:

```
1Ø FOR J=2 TO 1
2Ø PRINT "THIS SHOULD NOT BE PRINTED"
3Ø NEXT J
4Ø END
```

(vi) The initial, final, and step values are considered only when the loop is entered the first time so that they cannot later be altered. For example

```
5Ø FOR I=J TO K STEP L
6Ø LET L=L*2
7Ø LET K=K−1
8Ø NEXT I
```

If J, K, and L are 1, 10, and 1 the loop is repeated 10 times. The changes made to K and L inside the loop do not alter this.

(vii) The value of the loop variable itself can be changed inside the loop and this *will* affect its operation. For example

```
5Ø FOR I=1 TO 1Ø
6Ø LET I=I+1
7Ø NEXT I
```

is only repeated 5 times. Be sure that the difference between this and rule (vi) is understood.

(viii)   Computers can make slight errors when dealing with non-integers, and fail to hit an exact final value which could mean the loop will be executed an extra time. For example

```
1Ø LET  T=ATN( 1 )
2Ø LET  S=T/7
3Ø FOR  I=S  TO  T  STEP  S
4Ø PRINT  I
5Ø NEXT  I
```

might be executed 8 rather than 7 times because the seventh time S is added to I, it might fall fractionally short of T. If it does work, then this alternative probably will not:

```
3Ø FOR  I=T  TO  S  STEP  −S
```

(ix)   Loops can be abandoned; an IF . . . THEN or a GO TO within the loop could make the program leave it entirely.

(x)   A loop should never be jumped into from outside. Even if it works, it is usually unnecessary and is considered to be poor style.

(xi)   After leaving a loop the normal way, by dropping through the NEXT statement, the index has been incremented and is available. For example

```
1Ø FOR  I=1  TO  5
2Ø NEXT  I
3Ø PRINT  I
```

will print the value 6.

To match every FOR statement there must be a NEXT statement. The NEXT statement takes the form

> *line number* NEXT *variable*

which indicates the end of the loop. The named *variable* is the same loop index as appeared in the FOR statement.

Example   The factorial of an integer is the product of all integers up to and including the number. The factorial of 0 is 1. Here is a program segment to evaluate the factorial of N which works for 0 and any positive integer.

```
 80 REM EVALUATE FACTORIAL N
 90 REM INITIALISE FACTORIAL
100 LET F=1
110 REM FORM PRODUCT OF ALL INTEGERS TO N
120 IF N=0 THEN 160
130 FOR K=N TO 1 STEP −1
140 LET F=F*K
150 NEXT K
160 PRINT "FACTORIAL IS ";F
```

4   Nesting FOR and NEXT loops

Programs will often require several loops contained within one another. This is allowed by BASIC as long as they do not overlap, because if they did the intention of the program would be ambiguous. If they are correctly arranged they are said to be nested. Two examples serve to illustrate correct and incorrect arrangements.

Correct	**Incorrect**
The loops are 'nested'	The loops cross

```
10 FOR I=1 TO 10          10 FOR I=1 TO 10
   .                         .
   .                         .
   .                         .
30 FOR J=1 TO 5           30 FOR J=1 TO 5
   .                         .
   .                         .
   .                         .
50 NEXT J                 50 NEXT J
   .                         .
   .                         .
   .                         .
70 NEXT I                 70 NEXT J
```

The same variable cannot be used as a counter in nested loops, as follows:

```
10 FOR I=1 TO 10
30 FOR I=1 TO 5      not allowed
50 NEXT I
70 NEXT I
```

Example   Now we can do the sum of sums. On day D of Christmas, the number of gifts arriving is the sum of the integers from 1 to D. After twelve days of this, the grand total is the sum of all these sums:

```
10 REM THE SUM OF SUMS FROM 1 TO 12
20 LET S=0
30 FOR D=1 TO 12        60 NEXT G
40 FOR G=1 TO D         70 NEXT D
50 LET S= S+G           80 PRINT "THE SUM OF SUMS TO 12 IS ";S
                        90 END
```

Example   Here is a program which prints a table of compound interest return on 100 units invested at 6%, 7%, 8%, and 9% for up to 10 compoundings. The return r on principal p invested at $i\%$ for n periods is

$$r = p(1+i/100)^n$$

which is evaluated in nested loops for i from 6 to 9 and for n from 1 to 10.

```
100 REM PROGRAM TO PRINT INVESTMENT TABLE
110 PRINT "           TABLE OF RETURN ON INVESTMENT"
120 PRINT
130 PRINT "RATE ",6,7,8,9
140 REM REPEAT ON NEW LINE FOR 1 TO 10 PERIODS
150 FOR N=1 TO 10
160 PRINT "PERIOD ";N;                          200 NEXT I
170 REM PRINT ON ONE LINE FOR RATES 6 TO 9      210 PRINT
180 FOR I=6 TO 9                                220 NEXT N
190 PRINT 100*(1+I/100)∧N,                      230 END
```

5   Problems

Problem 7.1   The Maclaurin series for $\sin x$ is

$$\sin x = x - x^3/3! + x^5/5! - x^7/7! + \ldots$$

Write a program to evaluate 10 terms of this and compare it with the built-in SIN function for various values of x.

Problem 7.2   Now improve on the solution to 7.1. Be sure an efficient recurrence is being used. Before evaluating the series, scale x into the range $-\pi$ to π using a remainder. Limit the loop to however many repetitions are certain to produce a result correct to 5 figures for any value of x, but jump out of the loop earlier if the error indicated by the most recent term is small enough.

Problem 7.3   An example in this Unit shows how to calculate a factorial N!. The formulae for permutations and combinations are

$${}_nP_r$$ = number of arrangements (permutations) of n things taken r at a time

$$= \frac{n!}{(n-r)!}$$

$_nC_r$ = number of combinations of n things taken r at a time

$$= \frac{n!}{r!(n-r)!}$$

Write programs to calculate $_nC_r$ and $_nP_r$ where n and r are typed in.

Problem 7.4 Calculate and print nCr for $n = 0, 1, \ldots, 10$ and $r = 0, 1, \ldots, n$. Copy the PRINT arrangement from the investment table example to make all the results for a given n appear on the same line.

Problem 7.5 A prime number is one which has no factors other than itself or unity. For example 33 is not a prime number since it has factors 3 and 11. 3 and 11 are themselves prime numbers. Write a program to determine whether a number typed in is prime. To find out if a number i is prime, test for a zero remainder after division by every integer from 2 to i—if any is found, i is not prime.

Problem 7.6 Write a program to find and print all the primes less than 100.

Problem 7.7 Write a program to find all the prime factors of a number.

Problem 7.8 One method of finding the area under a curve is the trapezoidal rule; see Fig. 7.2.

The area a of the shaded trapezoid is

$$a = \frac{f(x_1) + f(x_2)}{2} \; (x_2 - x_1)$$

By dividing the range $0 < x < 1$ into N trapezoids, find the area under the curve $\text{EXP}(x^2/2)$ from $x = 0$ to $x = 1$. N is to be typed in. How big must N be for 0.1% accuracy?

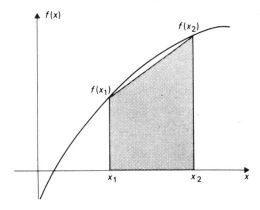

Fig. 7.2. Illustrating the trapezoidal rule.

UNIT 8
Printing and graph plotting

1 Introduction

The PRINT statement provides several ways of controlling the layout of lines of output. These days it is most likely that 'printing' is done on a screen rather than a printer, but the principles are the same. Some of these features have been demonstrated already, and the remainder are described here. In simple BASIC the placement and spacing af numerical output can be controlled only to a limited extent. However, in a different way BASIC is highly versatile in the facilities which allow graphs to be plotted and lines of output to be continued from one PRINT statement to the next.

2 Another look at the PRINT statement

In BASIC there are three means of controlling the alignment of printed information: the comma and semicolon as 'separators' and a special function, the TAB function. These are all used in the PRINT statement, whose general form can now be stated:

line number PRINT *quantity separator quantity separator*

where *quantity* can represent expressions of any complexity, character strings, or the special TAB function, and *separator* can be a comma or a semicolon.

Example

```
75 PRINT A,B+C,TAB(D);"CHARACTER STRING"
```

3 Printing with commas

Whenever quantities to be printed are separated by commas, BASIC divides the output line into a number of zones. The number of zones and their width will vary between computers, but would typically be 5 zones of 15 spaces if the printer or screen is wide enough. Numbers are always printed in the same zones regardless of their size or type of presentation. In this way BASIC can print tables whose columns will always be aligned.

Exercise Investigate the printing of numbers by BASIC:

(i) Look at how whole numbers (integers) are presented. Find out how large they are before they are printed in exponential format.

(ii) Look at non-integers and their printing in exponential format.

One new feature of printing with commas is the ability of BASIC to continue new statements on the same line, as in

```
6Ø  FOR  I = 1  TO  5
7Ø  PRINT  I,
8Ø  NEXT  I
9Ø  END
```

which will print the five values of I on the same line. To force a new line, use another PRINT statement, as in

```
1Ø  FOR  I = 1  TO  5
2Ø  FOR  J = 1  TO  5
3Ø  PRINT  I,
4Ø  NEXT  J
5Ø  PRINT
6Ø  NEXT  I
7Ø  END
```

Exercise   Try this new feature.

4   Printing with semicolons

If a semicolon is used in place of a comma in PRINT statements, then the output is squeezed together. The result is that more numbers can be printed on a line. Unfortunately the size of the zones varies according to the number of digits in the result. Therefore to get results laid out as tables, the comma is better. The semicolon is used when the printed results are intended to be squeezed together, for example when a numerical result follows a message. This has been used often in the examples in earlier chapters. To follow a message by a value, end the message with a space:

```
1Ø  PRINT  "THIS IS ";2
```

The other way around, the space is not necessary in most versions of BASIC, because a number ought to end with a space. This point should be checked:

```
1Ø  PRINT  2;"IS THERE A SPACE?"
```

Another use of the semicolon is in continuing printed output on the same line with several PRINT statements. If a semicolon is used as separator after the last quantity in a PRINT statement, then the next PRINT statement to be obeyed will continue on the same line, as in

```
10 FOR I = 1 TO 10
20 PRINT I;
30 NEXT I
40 END
```

A PRINT statement with nothing to print will cause a new line, as would any PRINT statement without a separator on the end:

```
10 FOR I = 1 TO 5
20 PRINT I;
30 FOR J = 1 TO 5
40 PRINT J;
50 NEXT J
60 PRINT
70 NEXT I
80 END
```

This same feature is useful when requesting input from the keyboard. A message can be given with a PRINT statement ending with a semicolon. The prompt and response to the INPUT statement will then follow on the same line. This makes a convenient and neat dialogue, as in

```
30 PRINT "WHAT IS N .. ";
40 INPUT N
```

Example   This program prints a little pyramid:

```
10 REM MAKE A PYRAMID — FIRST HALF
20 REM L IS THE LINE NUMBER
30 FOR L = 1 TO 12
40 REM C IS THE COLUMN NUMBER
50 FOR C = 1 TO L
60 PRINT "*";
70 NEXT C
80 REM MOVE TO NEXT LINE
90 PRINT
100 NEXT L
110 REM AND SO ON FOR THE SECOND HALF
120 FOR L = 11 TO 1 STEP —1
130 FOR C = 1 TO L
140 PRINT "*";
150 NEXT C
160 PRINT
170 NEXT L
180 END
```

Exercise   Try these features.

5   Print zoning—the TAB function

When the special TAB function and the semicolon are used together, a large measure of control over output zoning and graph plotting is available. TAB is a special function which can only be used in PRINT statements. It appears with a single argument such as TAB(x), where x could be an expression of any complexity. It causes the output to move along the printed line to the column given by the integer part of x, which should be an existing column number. TAB(x) is normally followed by a semicolon so that printing will begin in the next space, i.e. at column INT(x)+1. If TAB(x) were followed by a comma, then the output would move to the beginning of the next ordinary field which is usually wrong.

TAB can therefore place a number or a message exactly where it is wanted.

Exercise   Try the following example:

```
1Ø  FOR I=1 TO 1Ø
2Ø  PRINT TAB(I);I
3Ø  NEXT I
4Ø  END
```

It is important to know that the TAB function cannot move the printer backwards on the same line, and if it is attempted it will move to a new line. TAB always gives a column number, not a number of columns, so to move to column 60 from column 50, TAB(60) is used (not TAB(10)).

6   An example—displaying Pascal's triangle

Pascal's triangle is the arrangement of the coefficients of binomial expansions in triangular form as shown in Fig. 8.1.

$$_0C_0$$
$$_1C_0 \qquad _1C_1$$
$$_2C_0 \qquad _2C_1 \qquad _2C_2$$
$$_3C_0 \qquad _3C_1 \qquad _3C_2 \qquad _3C_3$$
$$_4C_0 \qquad _4C_1 \qquad _4C_2 \qquad _4C_3 \qquad _4C_4$$
$$_5C_0 \qquad _5C_1 \qquad _5C_2 \qquad _5C_3 \qquad _5C_4 \qquad _5C_5$$
$$_6C_0 \qquad _6C_1 \qquad _6C_2 \qquad _6C_3 \qquad _6C_4 \qquad _6C_5 \qquad _6C_6$$

Fig. 8.1. Pascal's Triangle.

The quantity $_nC_r$ was defined in Problem 7.3 as

$$_nC_r = \frac{n!}{r!(n-r)!}$$

from which in the search for efficiency, a recurrence can be found:

$$_nC_r = \frac{n-r+1}{r} \; _nC_{r-1}$$

which makes it unnecessary to find any factorials! To print the first line, send the printer back to column 35 before printing $_0C_0$. Using the TAB function, force each number to use only six spaces, and start each new line three spaces further back than the one before it. This way the output will be nicely lined up. Therefore line n begins at column $35-3n$ and the number $_nC_r$ is in column $35-3n+6r$. The complete program to display 10 lines of Pascal's triangle is:

```
100 REM A PROGRAM TO PRINT PASCAL'S TRIANGLE
110 REM N IS LINE NUMBER
120 FOR N=0 TO 9
130 REM PRINT THE FIRST VALUE ON EACH LINE
140 LET C=1
150 PRINT TAB(35-3*N);C;
160 REM NOW THE REMAINDER OF LINE N IF ANY
170 IF N=0 THEN 230
180 FOR R=1 TO N
190 LET C=C*(N-R+1)/R
200 PRINT TAB(35-3*N+6*R);C;
210 NEXT R
220 REM MOVE TO A NEW LINE
230 PRINT
240 NEXT N
250 END
```

Exercise   Run this program.

7   Line graphs

In output zoning, character strings can be treated like any other quantity. Therefore the TAB function can be used to move the display to a desired column where a character string can begin. This enables graphs to be plotted; the output is advanced to the correct place and a symbol is printed. To make the a graph fit the number of spaces available usually requires some scaling.

As an example, a straight line can be plotted easily by printing in column one of the first line, column two of the second, and so on. The program could be

```
10 FOR I=1 TO 10
20 PRINT TAB(I);"*"
30 NEXT I
40 END
```

The line of symbols that this makes is the graph. As a more complicated example, a cosine wave is displayed of amplitude 25 print positions and period 20 lines. If I is the line number from 0 to 19, then the function is

$$25 \cos \frac{2\pi I}{20}$$

but it must be displaced to prevent it from going off the screen to the left. The constant $2\pi/20$ is calculated in advance using the ATN function. Here is the program; note that the column number is 'rounded' by the addition of 0.5.

```
10 LET T=8*ATN(1)/20          40 NEXT I
20 FOR I=0 TO 19              50 END
30 PRINT TAB(25.5+25*COS(T*I));"*"
```

Exercise   Try these programs. The cosine graph is lying on its side.

8   Plotting bar graphs

A bar graph has a shaded or solid line drawn in each position. In BASIC a program calculates where to begin and how many symbols make up the bar before producing it in a FOR . . . NEXT loop. It is quite similar to the way we made our little pyramid. An example of a shaded straight line beginning in column 30 is:

```
10 FOR I=1 TO 10          50 NEXT J
20 PRINT TAB(30);         60 PRINT
30 FOR J=1 TO I           70 NEXT I
40 PRINT "*";             80 END
```

9   Problems

Problem 8.1   Plot a full cycle of a sine wave of amplitude 30 print positions and period 30 lines.

Problem 8.2   To a suitable scale plot the polynomial

$$f(x)=x^3 - 7.8x^2 + 18.5x - 11.3$$

Problem 8.3   Plot a full cycle of a cosine wave with the *x*-axis shown.

Problem 8.4   Plot a full cycle of a cosine wave and a sine wave together with the *x*-axis shown.

UNIT 9
Defining functions

1   Introduction

The standard built-in functions of BASIC have already been introduced. These cover the most common and important requirements for functions. In addition to these it is possible for a program to define its own functions in a restricted but useful way. Functions can shorten or simplify programs by replacing similar expressions which occur frequently in a program.

2   Defining functions—the DEF FN statement

A one-line function definition can be inserted in a BASIC program by the DEF FN statement:

line number DEF FN*a*(*variable*) = *expression*

The function name is FN*a*, where *a* can be any letter of the alphabet, so that the 26 available names are FNA, FNB, . . . , FNZ. A given name can only be defined once but can be referred to as often as is desired. The definition must come before the first reference to the function.

The *variable* in brackets is the argument of the function, and is called a 'dummy argument' because the variable name used in the DEF FN*a* statement is not the variable whose value is used when the function is referred to. The argument will normally appear in the right hand side *expression* but need not. When the function is used by a running program, the expression on the right hand side is evaluated with the value of the argument substituted for the variable in the function definition. A function can have one argument, or no arguments.

This may sound quite complicated but is really simple and will be illustrated by several examples.

Example   The area of a circle is πr^2, where *r* is the radius. A function can be defined to find the area of any circle by a statement like

$3\emptyset$ DEF FNC(R)=4*ATN(1)*R*R

which calculates the area of a circle given its radius as argument. Elsewhere in the same BASIC program this could be used, for example

```
45 PRINT "RADIUS ";X;" AREA ";FNC(X)
```

so that a complete program to print the areas of circles of radius 1.0, 1.1, . . . , 1.9, could be

```
1Ø REM PROGRAM TO FIND AREAS OF CIRCLES
2Ø REM DEFINE AREA FUNCTION
3Ø DEF FNC(R)=4*ATN(1)*R*R
4Ø REM NOW WORK OUT AREAS
5Ø FOR X=1.Ø TO 1.9 STEP Ø.1
6Ø PRINT "RADIUS ";X;" AREA ";FNC(X)
7Ø NEXT X
8Ø END
```

It should be clear how the function is defined using a dummy variable R and later referred to using an actual argument X.

The argument of a function need not be used. The standard for BASIC suggests that a function with no arguments can be used, but not all implementations allow this. Functions can refer to other functions but a function cannot refer to itself, nor can an endless loop of functions be permitted.

Example   The evaluation of π could be made by a function FNP:

```
25 DEF FNP=4*ATN(1)
```

in which case the previous function definition could itself use the defined function FNP:

```
3Ø DEF FNR(R)=FNP*R*R
```

Here the function FNP has no argument. If a particular computer does not like this, put any convenient variable name in the definition:

```
25 DEF FNP(Z)=4*ATN(1)
```

and when it is used

```
3Ø DEF FNR(R)=FNP(Z)*R*R
```

Example   The function FNT provides a true truncation of its argument:

```
6Ø DEF FNT(X)=SGN(X)*INT(ABS(X))
```

Example   The function FNR rounds its argument to the nearest integer:

```
7Ø DEF FNR(X)=INT(X+Ø.5)
```

On the right hand side of a function definition, variables may be used which are not arguments of the function. If this is done, the real value of the variable is used. To illustrate this, consider rounding to a particular accuracy as was illustrated in Unit 6.

Example   The function FND rounds its argument X after scaling by a scale factor S, so that S defines the precision of the scaling. After rounding, X is restored to its original size but is now rounded to the nearest S.

```
40 DEF FND(X)=(INT(X)/S+0.5)*S
```

so that with S = 100 rounding is to the nearest 100; with S = 0.01 rounding is to two decimal places.

Example   The function FNT throws two dice using the built-in RND function. In this little program, it is used to count the number of 7's that turn up in 100 throws.

```
10 REM THROW THE DICE 100 TIMES AND COUNT THE 7'S
20 DEF FNT=INT(RND*6+1)+INT(RND*6+1)
30 REM INITIALISE THE COUNT
40 LET N7=0          70 IF FNT<>7 THEN 100
50 REM NOW THROW     80 REM YES, WE HAVE A 7
60 FOR T=1 TO 100    90 LET N7=N7+1
                     100 NEXT T
                     110 PRINT "AFTER 100 THROWS WE HAVE ";N7;" SEVENS"
                     120 END
```

3   Problems

Problem 9.1   Define functions for hyperbolic sine, cosine, and tangent and plot them over the range $-2 < x < 2$.

$$\sinh x = \frac{e^x - e^{-x}}{2} \qquad \cosh x = \frac{e^x + e^{-x}}{2} \qquad \tanh x = \frac{\sinh x}{\cosh x}$$

Problem 9.2   Define a function for arc sine using a suitable range of angles.

Problem 9.3   Define a function for arc cosine using a suitable range of angles.

Problem 9.4   Define a function to transfer the sign of a variable S to the function argument. Try to make it work for S = 0.

Problem 9.5   Define a function to find the remainder when N, the function argument, is divided by D. Use this to convert

33	to base 7	7600	to base 6
32 767	to base 5	5100	to base 8

UNIT 10
Working with lists

1 Introduction

Most computing languages provide what is called an array facility; a means of organising a list of values under only one variable name. A program can refer to any member of the list by the use of a subscript, and by varying the value of the subscript a common calculation can be applied throughout the list.

2 Lists and subscripts

In BASIC an ordered set of values can be given one variable name and treated as a list. A particular member of the list can be selected by the use of a subscript. BASIC automatically recognises a variable as a list if it is used with a subscript, and the subscript itself can be any expression. The name of a list can only be a single letter.

Examples

A(3)	refers to the third entry in the list called A
B(I+J)	refers to the (I+J)th entry in the list called B

A subscript can be any expression, but it is obvious that it has to be interpreted as a positive integer. If the value of the subscript is not an integer, it should be rounded to the nearest integer by the computer. However some BASIC implementations truncate to the next lowest integer rather than rounding. To ensure that a program works on all computers, use only integer values as subscripts.

Example

    C(3.75)   refers to entry number four in the list called C.

BASIC checks every subscript as it is used and if subscripts occur which are too small or too large the program will not be allowed to continue. The BASIC standard recommends that the lowest permitted subscript should be 0, but unfortunately a number of implementations have 1 as the smallest subscript. To make a program transportable, consider that 1 is the lowest subscript.

The same variable name should not be used in both subscripted and unsubscripted form in a program. Unsubscripted variables of the kind used in earlier Units are properly called simple variables.

The use of lists in programs is demonstrated by a series of examples.

Example Defining and printing a list.

A convenient way of assigning values to a list in advance is described in Unit 12. In the meantime less convenient ways are used. Suppose in a prison with four cells, each prisoner has been given a prisoner number. The set of prisoner numbers could form a list in which subscripts correspond to the numbering of the cells, as illustrated by Fig. 10.1.

The list is described as

	Subscript		Value
The prisoner in cell	1	is	631
The prisoner in cell	2	is	127
The prisoner in cell	3	is	458
The prisoner in cell	4	is	390

In a BASIC program, the list of prisoner numbers could be called N. Subscripts 1 to 4 select different cells, and the prisoner numbers are $N(1)$, $N(2)$, $N(3)$ and $N(4)$. The following program reads in the prisoner numbers one at a time and prints them out again. In a FOR . . . NEXT loop the INPUT statement at line 30 refers to the cell numbers one at a time with subscript I. At line 60 the subscripted variable $N(J)$ prints them as J varies.

```
10 PRINT "TYPE IN THE PRISONER NUMBERS ONE AT A TIME"
20 FOR I=1 TO 4
30 INPUT N(I)
40 NEXT I
50 FOR J=4 TO 1 STEP −1                                    70 NEXT J
60 PRINT "THE PRISONER IN CELL ";J;" IS NUMBER ";N(J)      80 END
```

CELL No.1   CELL No.2   CELL No.3   CELL No.4

Fig. 10.1. A list of prisoners.

Example Suppose now a search is to be made for the highest prisoner number. To do this a simple variable H is set aside and given a prisoner number from the list—$N(1)$. H is then compared with each remaining prisoner number in turn. Whenever a higher number than H is found, this value replaces H. At the end H will hold the highest number. This is added on to the previous example:

```
8Ø REM NOW SEARCH FOR THE HIGHEST NUMBER
9Ø LET H=N(1)
1ØØ FOR I=2 TO 4                    12Ø LET H=N(J)
11Ø IF H>=N(J) THEN 13Ø            13Ø NEXT I
                                    14Ø PRINT "THE HIGHEST NUMBER IS ";H
                                    15Ø END
```

Exercise Draw a flowchart for this program and find the deliberate error. Correct it and try the program. Modify it to find the lowest prisoner number. Further modify it to record and print the cell number of this prisoner as well.

Example Additional arrays can be defined to give additional facts about the prisoners. The length of sentence and the ages on arrival might also be of interest, defined as new arrays A and L, for example

Cell	1	2	3	4
Prisoner number	631	127	458	390
Sentence	99	1	53	30
Age on arrival	40	44	35	21

The following part program is used to define these:

```
1Ø PRINT "INPUT PRISONER NO., SENTENCE, AND AGE"
2Ø FOR I=1 TO 4
3Ø INPUT N(I),L(I),A(I)
4Ø NEXT I
```

Problems using this data are found at the end of this Unit.

3   Longer lists—the DIM statement

In the previous examples the space taken up by a list has been ignored. BASIC should assume that a list contains as many as 11 values (for the subscripts 0 to 10). Unfortunately some implementations only allow for subscripts 1 to 10. The OPTION statement can be used to tell a system what the lowest subscript should be:

line number OPTION BASE 0 *or* 1

If no OPTION is given, an up-to-date version of BASIC should assume that the minimum is 0. This, however, is an area of confusion because:

(i) Some versions of BASIC do not assume any space for arrays and insist on the DIM statement.

(ii) Versions of BASIC that do assume array space might set aside 11 spaces (for subscripts 0 to 10) or they might set aside only 10 (for subscripts 1 to 10).

(iii) Versions of BASIC that set aside array space might not have the OPTION statement.

The safest thing is to assume the minimum is 1, and always give a DIM statement, which has to be done anyway if the largest subscript is greater than 10. All versions of BASIC use the DIM statement to specify the largest subscript to be used with particular arrays.

The DIM statement specifies the size of lists:

> *line number* DIM *name*(*size*), *name*(*size*), . . .

The *size* specifies the largest subscript that will ever be used by the program for the list variable *name*. The DIM statement can appear anywhere in the program before the lists it names are first used. Like the REM or DEF FN statements, a running program takes no action when it is reached. It is simply for the information of BASIC. Most programmers put it at the beginning for clarity. A particular variable name should appear in only one DIM statement.

Examples

        5 DIM N(4),L(4),A(4)

specifies that the largest subscript for the lists A, L, and N is 4. This statement could have appeared in the previous example and would save space.

        63 DIM X7(2ØØ)

reserves 200 spaces for a list called X7.

Example   An array can be used to count the number of times each outcome arises when throwing dice many times. Each member of the array is a counter, and happily its subscript is also the outcome that it is used to count. The result is an 'histogram'.

```
1Ø REM A HISTOGRAM OF DICE THROWING
2Ø DIM H(12)
3Ø DEF FNT=INT(RND*6+1)+INT(RND*6+1)
4Ø REM INITIALISE THE COUNTERS
5Ø FOR I=1 TO 12
6Ø LET H(I)=Ø
7Ø NEXT I
8Ø PRINT "HOW MANY THROWS SHALL I DO .. ";
9Ø INPUT N
1ØØ REM THROW N TIMES, COUNTING ALL OCCURRENCES
11Ø FOR T=1 TØ N
12Ø LET D=FNT
13Ø LET H(D)=H(D)+1          15Ø REM SHOW THE RESULT
14Ø NEXT T                   16Ø PRINT
                            17Ø FOR I=2 TO 12
```

```
18Ø PRINT "RESULT ";I;" OCCURRED ";H(I);" TIMES"
19Ø NEXT I
2ØØ END
```

Exercise Using the same program, print the histogram as a bar graph. You can make a different outcome occur each time if you RANDOMIZE anywhere before line 110.

4 Shuffling lists

In calculations using simple variable names, the idea of replacing one variable by a new value after calculation has occurred frequently, for example in the recurrence relationship of a series evaluation. The same concept also applies to list calculations, except that the replacements are often done in some ordered way within the list. As an illustration the same prisoners could be required to rotate their cells, so that each moves down one cell number, except the prisoner in cell 1, who moves to cell 4.

In a computer program only one value can be moved at a time; in the prison analogy this would correspond to having only one guard to move the prisoners. The sequence of operations would be:

The prisoner in cell 1 moves out temporarily.
The old prisoner in cell 2 becomes the new prisoner in cell 1.
The old prisoner in cell 3 becomes the new prisoner in cell 2.
The old prisoner in cell 4 becomes the new prisoner in cell 3.

and finally

The old prisoner in cell 1 becomes the new prisoner in cell 4.

The effect of this reshuffling is:

Before		**After**	
Cell	Prisoner	Cell	Prisoner
1	631	1	127
2	127	2	458
3	458	3	390
4	390	4	631

If there are other arrays associated with the original order, then these should also be shuffled. The prisoners moving into cells 1 and 3 would not be happy if they inherited the previous inmate's sentence.

A program segment which moves the prisoners and keeps track of their sentence could be:

```
30 REM STORE PRISONER FROM CELL 1 TEMPORARILY
40 LET X1=N(1)
50 LET X2=L(1)
60 REM MOVE THE OTHERS DOWN ONE CELL
70 FOR I=1 TO 3
80 LET N(I)=N(I+1)        110 REM PUT TEMPORARY PRISONER IN CELL 4
90 LET L(I)=L(I+1)        120 LET N(4)=X1
100 NEXT I                130 LET L(4)=X2
```

A very common and embarrassing program error arises if the shuffle is done in the wrong sequence. The prisoners have been moved down in ascending cell order. If they had moved down in descending order, then the old prisoner in cell 4 would be in cells 1, 2, and 3, and it would be some time before the other two were missed. Thus the shuffle can be performed downwards in ascending order, in which case the first convict goes into temporary storage. Alternatively they can be moved upwards in descending order in which case the temporary storage is used for the last convict.

5   Problems

Problem 10.1   Using the data for prisoner numbers, sentences and ages, write a program to find:

(i)   the cell number of the prisoner with the shortest unexpired sentence;
(ii)   the prisoner number of the oldest prisoner;
(iii) the sentence of the prisoner whose age is closest to the mean.

Problem 10.2   In the same jail the policy is to release a prisoner for good behaviour when he has either served half his sentence rounded up to the nearest year or has reached the age of 70. Write a program to determine how many years each will serve assuming good behaviour.

Problem 10.3   The conversion of numbers from base 10 to another base can now be organised properly using a list to hold the digits of the result. As before, the digits are found in reverse order by the remainders after successive division. Now they can be saved in the correct order by placing them backwards in the list. Alternatively the list of results could be printed in reverse order. Before writing the program, work out how long a list is needed, assuming that the largest decimal number is 10000 and that the smallest base is 2.

Example   Find 131 to base 7.

Successive division by 7: $131/7 = 18$ remainder 5
 $18/7\ = 2$ remainder 4
 $2/7\ = 0$ remainder 2
Answer: 245

UNIT 11
Character strings

1 Introduction

This Unit describes how BASIC can manipulate strings of alphabetic characters. Character string constants have been used as messages in PRINT statements in this text. Now it will be seen that these can be put to several further uses. The string variable facility allows messages to be used in several other statements of BASIC. Some of the more restricted forms of BASIC will allow only a few of the operations described here, and by contrast a few extended versions of BASIC offer a range of string manipulation functions which are not described here. However if the BASIC is standard, it should conform to this description.

2 Messages as constants or variables

A string constant is any series of acceptable symbols enclosed by quotation marks, and can include letters, numeric digits, blanks, and a number of other characters. The only BASIC symbol not permitted is the quotation mark itself, because it is used to delimit the constant. In the BASIC statement

```
77 PRINT "THIS IS A STRING CONSTANT"
```

the message 'THIS IS A STRING CONSTANT' is a string constant.

A string variable is given one of 26 special names which are reserved for this use. These consist of a letter and the dollar sign $. Therefore the names available are

```
A$, B$, . . ., Z$
```

String variables can be subscripted. Therefore the statement

```
1Ø DIM A$(75)
```

defines a string list or array with 75 entries.

3 Using character strings in BASIC statements

Meaningful operations on character strings can be performed by many of the statements of BASIC. The use of string constants in the PRINT statement is familiar, and other uses are outlined here.

(a)   LET

The LET statement may contain a string variable on the left hand side, and a string variable or constant on the right hand side. However, string expressions cannot replace ordinary variables and numeric expressions cannot replace string variables. Thus the use of LET with strings in the minimum standard BASIC is restricted to

> *line number* LET *string*   = *string variable*
> *variable*   or *constant*

Note, however, that subscripted forms are allowed.

Example

```
10 LET A$=B$
20 LET C$="MUD IN YOUR EYE"
30 LET  D$=E$(I+3*J)
40 LET F$(L)="YOUR GRANDMOTHER WEARS ARMY BOOTS"
```

(b)   PRINT

The PRINT statement can include either string constants or string variables. The comma and semicolon used as delimiters have the usual meaning.

Example

```
10 LET M$="DISGUSTING"
20 PRINT "TODAY'S MESSAGE IS ";M$
```

(c)   INPUT

The INPUT statement can include string variables. The message typed in response to the INPUT request does not need quotation marks as long as it contains only letters, digits, spaces, and the symbols minus, period (decimal point), and plus. The string has to have quotation marks if it includes other symbols such as the comma, which it would otherwise confuse with the commas separating input values.

Exercise   Experiment with

```
10 INPUT A$,B$
20 PRINT A$,B$
30 END
```

paying particular attention to the rules about quotation marks outlined above.

Note that when asking for character input, the command which interrupts the computer (such as STOP or BREAK) may not work. The program

```
1Ø  INPUT  A$        3Ø  GO  TO  1Ø
2Ø  PRINT  A$        4Ø  END
```

could present difficulties. If asking for string input in an endless loop it would be wise to check for the stop message, as

```
15  IF  A$="STOP"  THEN  4Ø
```

See the IF . . . THEN statement which follows.

(d) IF . . . THEN

A very useful application of string variables is in the IF . . . THEN statement. Two strings can be compared as

line number **IF** *string   relational   string* **THEN** *line number*
                              operator

Standard BASIC only allows the relational operators = or <> with strings, the tests for equality or otherwise. However, many versions of BASIC will also permit other comparisons which are useful for putting things into alphabetical order, < for example. If this is allowed, the statement

```
25Ø  IF  "ABC"<B$(I)  THEN  3ØØ
```

will compare the string constant 'ABC' with the list entry B$(I). If 'ABC' is earlier in alphabetical order than B$(I) the jump occurs to line 300. Usually a string comparison is done on the basis of alphabetical order: it is not necessary for the strings to be of the same length, as the following examples show.

"ABC"	is greater than	"ABB"
	or	"AB"
"ABC"	is equal to	"ABC"
"ABC"	is less than	"ABD"
	or	"ABCA"
	or	"ABC " (Note the blank.)

Comparison between strings and arithmetic expressions is not permitted.

(e) DIM

String variables may be used with subscripts and so can form lists. As with ordinary variables, the use must be consistent. If not given explicitly, the maximum size is taken as 10. It will be seen later that arrays can have one, two, or three subscripts and strings are not an exception.

(f)   DATA and READ

These statements are introduced in the next Unit and, as will be seen, they can be used with strings.

Example   Here is a program which finds all the 24 anagrams of the word DAVE. To do it, you start with D as the first letter and find all the anagrams of AVE. Then you rotate DAVE into AVED, and so on. Can you follow all the switching?

```
1ØØ REM ALL THE ANAGRAMS OF DAVE
11Ø LET D$="D"
12Ø LET A$="A"
13Ø LET V$="V"                      23Ø      REM SWITCH A$ WITH V$
14Ø LET E$="E"                      24Ø      LET V$=A$
15Ø FOR I=1 TO 4                    25Ø      LET A$=T$
16Ø    FOR J=1 TO 3                 26Ø   NEXT J
17Ø      PRINT D$;A$;V$;E$          27Ø   REM ROTATE  —  T$ ALREADY HOLDS A$
18Ø      REM SWITCH V$ WITH E$      28Ø   LET A$=V$
19Ø      LET T$=E$                  29Ø   LET V$=E$
2ØØ      LET E$=V$                  3ØØ   LET E$=D$
21Ø      LET V$=T$                  31Ø   LET D$=T$
22Ø      PRINT D$;A$;V$;E$          32Ø NEXT I
                                    33Ø END
```

Exercise   How would you do a five letter word?

4   Problems

Problem 11.1   Write a program which translates integer numbers into their English digits. (Remainders again—use a string array for the words.)

Example: 123 is ONE TWO THREE

Problem 11.2   Write a program which sorts a list into alphabetical order. This requires IF statements to test for alphabetical ordering which most implementations of BASIC support, but not all.

Problem 11.3   Write a program to assist an author in preparing an index. He goes through his book at the keyboard, typing in the headings and page numbers as they are encountered. When he is finished, he types in 'FINISHED', assuming this message will not occur in the index. The program then sorts his lists according to the alphabetical order of the headings. The same heading may occur several times. The index is then printed with one entry for each heading. If there are repeated entries for a heading, the page numbers appear in order on one line of the output. The author will, of course, further edit this index.

UNIT 12
Defining values in advance

1 Introduction

Several times in earlier units it was necessary to give a program data values that were known in advance by the laborious method of typing them in whenever the program was run, or through a long series of LET statements. The assignment of sentences and ages to the prisoners in Unit 10 was one example, and in the problems with strings the same difficulty will have arisen. This unit describes the convenient way of setting up data constants in a program once and for all.

2 Assigning values—the DATA, READ, and RESTORE statements

BASIC allows a list of constants to be set aside in the computer in the DATA statement, and these values can be assigned to any variable using the READ statement. This facility eliminates the need to enter known constants every time a program is run.

The DATA statement has the form:

line number DATA *constant, constant, ...*

The DATA statement itself has no effect in a running BASIC program. In this it resembles several other statements encountered earlier, including the DIM statement. It is a statement for the information of BASIC, and it causes the *constants* to be stored in the computer, where they can be retrieved by a READ statement when the program is run. Any number of DATA statements can be included in a program and they can be put anywhere. If there are several, their order is important, however. The *constants* can be numbers in any of the usual BASIC forms, or they can be string constants as will be seen later.

An example of a DATA statement is

    1∅ DATA 38.2,1∅.5,−9.6

The READ statement is used to assign values from the DATA statement to the desired variables. It is written as

line number READ *variable, variable, ...*

This statement is acted upon by a running program. Values are assigned to the named *variables* from the DATA statements in order and in one-to-one correspondence with the requirements of the READ statement. For example, consider the program

```
1Ø DATA 38.2,1Ø.5,-9.6
2Ø READ A,B,C
3Ø PRINT A,B,C
4Ø END
```

In this program, A will be assigned the value 38.2, B the value 10.5, and C will be −9.6.

Successive READ statements in the running program carry on through the DATA list. Therefore if only part of a DATA statement is used by a given READ, then the next READ starts with the next value. In effect a pointer moves through the DATA constants as values are requested by READ statements.

Consider the program

```
1Ø DATA 38.2,1Ø.5,-9.6
2Ø FOR I=1 TO 3
3Ø READ Z
4Ø PRINT Z
5Ø NEXT I
6Ø END
```

Here, the DATA pointer is initially at the beginning of the list:

next value
☞
38.2   10.5   −9.6

When I = 1, the statement READ Z assigns 38.2 to Z and moves the pointer along:

next value
☞
38.2   10.5   −9.6

so that when I = 2, 10.5 is assigned to Z and the pointer moves again:

next value
☞
38.2   10.5   −9.6

and the final request assigns Z to be −9.6.

Similarly, if more variables are requested by one READ statement than are given by one DATA statement, the next DATA statement according to line number is taken. Thus the order of DATA statements is important because the DATA area is made up from the DATA statements taken in order. It is wrong to ask for more constants than are present in all the DATA statements.

Example

```
1Ø DATA 38.2          6Ø PRINT Z
2Ø FOR I=1 TO 3       7Ø DATA 4E31
3Ø DATA 1Ø.5          8Ø NEXT I
4Ø READ Z             9Ø DATA 75
5Ø DATA −9.6          1ØØ END
```

This example indicates how the DATA statements can be broken up, but is also an example of how to make a program hard to read. This is not good style.

The RESTORE statement returns the pointer to the beginning of the DATA area, so that all the given data can be re-used. In most versions of BASIC, there is no direct means of returning to the middle of the DATA list, but it is possible to return to the beginning with RESTORE and read through to the desired place, for example in a FOR ... NEXT loop.

RESTORE has the form:

line number RESTORE

Exercise Try the following program:

```
1Ø DATA 1,2,3
2Ø FOR J=1 TO 2       6Ø NEXT I
3Ø FOR I=1 TO 3       7Ø RESTORE
4Ø READ X             8Ø NEXT J
5Ø PRINT X;           9Ø END
```

The behaviour of the pointer in this program is then:

First:

```
            ☞
J = 1      1   2   3
I = 1
                ☞
J = 1      1   2   3
I = 2
                    ☞
J = 1      1   2   3
I = 3
```

RESTORE

J = 2   1   2   3
I = 1

J = 2   1   2   3
I = 2

J = 2   1   2   3
I = 3

RESTORE

         1   2   3

3   Assigning values to an array

Values are assigned to an array variable in much the same way as to any other, except that subscripts have to be used. To fill an array from the DATA area, FOR . . . NEXT loops must therefore be used.

Examples

```
1Ø DATA 38.2,1Ø.5,-9.6
2Ø FOR I=1 TO 3
3Ø READ X(I)
4Ø NEXT I
5Ø PRINT X(1),X(2),X(3)
6Ø END
```

```
1Ø DATA 38.2
2Ø FOR I=1 TO 3
3Ø DATA 1Ø.5
4Ø READ X(I)
5Ø DATA -9.6
6Ø NEXT I
7Ø PRINT X(1),X(2),X(3)
8Ø END
```

As before, the second example illustrates the point but is poor style.

4   Assigning values to string variables

String constants can be included in DATA statements, for example

```
1Ø DATA 1ØØ,STRING,2ØØ,CONSTANT
```

stores the string constants 'STRING' and 'CONSTANT' in the DATA area alongside the numeric values. There are no quotation marks in this example. However quotation marks have to be used sometimes. There is a great variation among computers on this point. The standard for BASIC suggests an arrangement which is unfortunately not followed. To make a program transportable, the safest thing would be always to use quotes, particularly if the string contains anything other than letters.

Examples

```
1Ø DATA STRING,CONSTANT
```

defines two string constants 'STRING' and 'CONSTANT' without quotation marks. Usually this would be safe.

```
1Ø DATA "STRING,CONSTANT"
```

defines one string constant, 'STRING,CONSTANT' which includes a comma.

```
1Ø DATA "+FIVE"," GO","... AND THEN","123 ZOOM"
```

defines a number of string constants which probably require the quotation marks.

The BASIC standard does not provide for quotation marks themselves to appear in strings. However, most versions of BASIC in the real world would accept that two quotes together indicate a quote, for example

to get " put ""

so that a PRINT statement might have

```
5Ø PRINT " TO GET "" PUT """"""
```

The READ statement can obviously include string variable names which must correspond in position with string constants in the DATA list.

Example

```
1Ø DATA 1ØØ,"STRING ",2ØØ,CONSTANT
2Ø READ X,A$,Y,B$
3Ø PRINT A$;B$
4Ø END
```

Example Using a string array to hold the result, a decimal number can readily be converted into the hexadecimal number system (base 16) in which the digits from 0 to 15 are represented as 0 to 9 followed by A to F. This is a very useful number system in computers. In the program, the symbols for the hexadecimal digits are copied into the array H$. Then, the remainder after dividing by 16 is found, which tells us where to find the digit in H$. It is written to use OPTION BASE 1 which is always safe.

```
1ØØ REM DECIMAL TO HEXADECIMAL
11Ø DIM H$(16),A$(4)
12Ø DATA "Ø","1","2","3","4","5","6","7"
13Ø DATA "8","9","A","B","C","D","E","F"
14Ø REM READ THE HEX DIGITS INTO H$
15Ø FOR K=1 TO 16
```

```
16Ø READ H$(K)
17Ø NEXT K
18Ø PRINT "ENTER A DECIMAL NUMBER FROM Ø TO 65535"
19Ø INPUT N
2ØØ REM CONVERT IT
21Ø FOR K=1 TO 4
22Ø LET D=N-INT(N/16)*16
23Ø LET N=INT(N/16)
24Ø LET A$(K)=H$(D+1)
25Ø NEXT K
26Ø REM PRINT THE RESULT
27Ø PRINT "IN HEXADECIMAL THAT IS ";
28Ø FOR K=1 TO 4
29Ø PRINT A$(5-K);              31Ø PRINT
3ØØ NEXT K                      32Ø END
```

5   Problems

Problem 12.1   Looking up an entry in a table is a very common requirement, especially in the commercial world. Establish a list of numbers by a DATA statement and make a program to search the list for a particular entry that may or may not appear.

Problem 12.2   Write a program to translate an integer into English digits. This time the digits can be stored in a DATA area. For example, 123 is ONE TWO THREE.

Problem 12.3   A company payroll is defined in DATA statements. The first one tells how many employees there are. There is then one further statement for each employee defining among other things their name and salary. Write a program to read the list, which is in no particular order, and print two summaries, one in alphabetical order and the other in reverse order of earnings. If you feel ambitious, tax them heavily for all kinds of things and print their miserably small monthly cheques.

Problem 12.4   The solution to Problem 12.1 will have involved searching the list entirely each time. A 'binary search' is much more efficient. Suppose there is a prison with 16 inmates in it. Define their cell numbers, ages and sentences in order of prisoner number. Write a program which enables the Warden to type in a prisoner number and retrieve the information about the prisoner and his probable real sentence for good behaviour as defined in Problem 10.2. Do this by a 'binary search'. First the prisoner number is compared with the number 8 in the list to find which half it is in (or it might by luck be the eighth). Then it is compared with number 4 or 12 to find which quarter it is in, and so on. For example if prisoner number 53 was the third in the list, the program would decide on first half, first quarter, second eighth and finally find him. In a 16 person prison it can never take more than 4 tries to locate a prisoner.

UNIT 13

Subroutines

1 Introduction

Properly used, the subroutine is another facility which can improve the structure of a program. With the function definition statement described in Unit 9, a one line calculation could be expressed as a function and then referred to throughout a program. With subroutines, a computation of any length and complexity can be written as a separate unit and then used at will in a program.

2 Defining subroutines—the GOSUB and RETURN statements

A subroutine is a separate program module not restricted to one line. It is written as a self-contained unit, starting at some line number which does not occur elsewhere, and containing its own line numbers in order. The program calls for the subroutine explicitly in a GOSUB statement, and to get back from the subroutine the RETURN statement is necessary.

Example   A subroutine is required to evaluate the factorial of a number. Suppose N9 is a positive integer or zero, and its factorial is required. The factorial of N9 is the product of all the integers from 1 to N9 and the factorial of zero is 1. A subroutine is written starting at line 2000 to work out this product in a FOR . . . NEXT loop:

```
2000 REM SUBROUTINE TO FIND FACTORIAL OF N9
2010 REM ANSWER IN N8, I9 IS USED
2020 LET N8=1
2030 IF N9<2 THEN 2070
2040 FOR I9=N9 TO 2 STEP −1
2050 LET N8=N8*I9
2060 NEXT I9
2070 RETURN
2080 END
```

This subroutine always finds the factorial of N9 and returns the answer as N8. It will work for any positive or zero N9. For negative N9 the answer 1 is returned. Variable I9 is used in the calculation. To use this subroutine as part of a BASIC program care must be taken that I9, N8, and N9 are not used in a conflicting way because the same variables are shared by all parts of the program.

A program to make use of this subroutine could be:

```
1Ø REM THIS IS A PROGRAM TO FIND THE FACTORIALS
2Ø REM OF NUMBERS TYPED IN AT THE KEYBOARD
3Ø REM
4Ø REM REQUEST INPUT
5Ø PRINT "NUMBER WHOSE FACTORIAL IS REQUIRED";
6Ø INPUT N9
7Ø GOSUB 2ØØØ
8Ø PRINT "FACTORIAL ";N9;" IS ";N8
9Ø GO TO 5Ø
```

When these are used together, the subroutine is called at line 70 by the GOSUB statement. On its completion at line 2060, the subroutine comes back with the RETURN statement.

The power of the subroutine lies in its ability to return to the place from which it was called. It could be called from a program several times, or from another subroutine, or both. However, a subroutine should not call itself, and an endless loop of subroutines should not be established.

Exercise   Run this program. Notice the semicolon in line 50.

The statements provided for subroutine usage are:

>   *line number a* GOSUB *line number b*

This statement causes a jump to a subroutine at *line number b*.

>   *line number b* RETURN

This statement sends the program back to the line following the GOSUB which called it.

3   Terminating programs—the STOP statement

Before subroutines were introduced, the END statement was sufficient both to end and terminate the program. The END statement is still required to be the highest numbered line in a BASIC program, subroutines and all. Therefore a program must always end with one and only one END statement. The STOP statement is available to stop or terminate the running of a program and can be put anywhere in the program. It is simply

>   *line number* STOP

and when it is encountered, execution of the program stops. Thus in the example of section 2, line 90 could have been a STOP statement.

Example   This little subroutine arranges an array R of numbers into order from smallest to largest. The method used is called bubble sorting. On each pass through the array, larger values are carried along, like bubbles rising to the top. This can be put into any program to sort numbers as long as you remember that the subroutine obliterates variables R6, R7 and R8, as well as rearranging the table R.

```
1000 REM BUBBLE SORTING ROUTINE        1080    LET R6=R(R7)
1010 REM SORTS R9 MEMBERS OF ARRAY R   1090    LET R(R7)=R(R7+1)
1020 REM USES VARIABLES R6, R7, R8     1100    LET R(R7+1)=R6
1030 LET R8=R9                         1110    LET R6=R7
1040 LET R6=1                          1120 NEXT R7
1050 FOR R7=1 TO R8-1                   1130 LET R8=R6
1060     IF R(R7)<R(R7+1) THEN 1120     1140 IF R8<>1 THEN 1040
1070     REM SWITCH TWO NUMBERS         1150 RETURN
```

4 An example

A program to find the area under a curve is the kind of requirement which is suitable for organisation as a subroutine. The algorithm is easily separated in any program which will use it, and it is likely that a good one would be useful to many people.

The trapezoidal rule which was illustrated in Fig. 7.2 is a simple method for finding the area under a curve. The area of the shaded trapezoid was

$$area = \frac{[f(x_1) + f(x_2)]}{2} (x_2 - x_1)$$

If a larger number of trapezoids are taken, then the area is obtained by summation. In Fig. 13.1 a curve has been divided into N9 trapezoids between X8 and X9, and here

$$area = H9 * \frac{[f(X8) + f(X9)]}{2} + f(X8+H9) + f(X8 + 2*H9)$$
$$+ \ldots + f(X8+(N9-1)*H9)$$

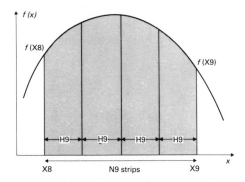

Fig. 13.1. Illustrating the trapezoidal rule with many segments.

where

$$H9 = \frac{X9 - X8}{N9}$$

A BASIC subroutine which finds the area under a curve which is defined by FNZ(X) between the limits X8 and X9 using N9 strips is given below. To use this, it is necessary to define the function FNZ and call the subroutine with the desired values of X8, X9 and N9 already assigned. The subroutine makes use of the variable S9 for summation, I9 for counting, and H9 for strip width. The subroutine assumes correct values of X8, X9, and N9. It will work for any integer N9 greater than 0.

```
6000 REM AREA UNDER A CURVE FNZ BY TRAPEZOID RULE
6010 REM FROM X8 TO X9 IN N9 STRIPS
6020 REM VARIABLES S9, I9 AND H9 ARE USED
6030 REM
6040 REM CALCULATE STRIP WIDTH        6080 REM DO REMAINING SUM
6050 LET  H9=(X9-X8)/N9               6090 FOR I9=N9-1 TO 1 STEP -1
6060 REM END VALUES OF SUM            6100 LET S9=S9+FNZ(X8+I9*H9)
6070 LET S9=0.5*(FNZ(X8)+FNZ(X9))     6110 NEXT I9
                                      6120 REM MULTIPLY BY H9 AND RETURN
                                      6130 LET S9=S9*H9
                                      6140 RETURN
```

Exercise   Write a program to use this subroutine which accepts X8, X9, and N9 in an INPUT statement and find the area under

$$\frac{1}{\sqrt{2\pi}} \exp(-x^2/2)$$

between $x = 0$ and $x = 1$. How many strips are required to give an answer which is correct to 4 decimal places?

Exercise   Improve the safety of the subroutine by making it check for a sensible value of N9 and ensuring that X9 > X8.

5   Problems

Problem 13.1   Write a subroutine to make a single line of a bar graph by shading from columns C8 to C9 or C9 to C8, depending on which is greater. Write another subroutine which draws a bar graph of a function FNX between X8 and X9 in steps using scale factor K9 and offset O9. This subroutine should call on the first one to do the actual drawing. Using these draw a shaded graph of a cosine.

Problem 13.2   Write a subroutine which scans the first L9 entries in a list Q9, and finds the largest value M9 and its position N9.

Problem 13.3   Write a subroutine which sorts a string list A\$ of length L9 into alphabetical order.

Problem 13.4   Write a subroutine to solve the equation

$$\text{FNY}(X) \ = \ \emptyset$$

by Newton's method given an initial guess X9. The subroutine should return the answer R9 when the latest step size is less than E9. Use this to find the square root of 2.

Problem 13.5   Another method of area calculation is known as Simpson's rule, Fig. 13.2. Here two adjoining segments are fitted by a parabolic curve and the shaded area *a* is

$$a \ = \ \frac{h}{3} \ [f(x_1) + 4f(x_2) + f(x_3)]$$

Write a subroutine to divide the range from X8 to X9 of a function FNZ into 2*N9 strips and find the area by Simpson's rule. Using this calculate the area under

$$f(x) = \frac{1}{\sqrt{2\pi}} \exp(-x^2/2)$$

between $x = 0$ and $x = 1$. Find out how many strips are required for 4 decimal places of accuracy. How does the number required compare with the trapezoidal rule?

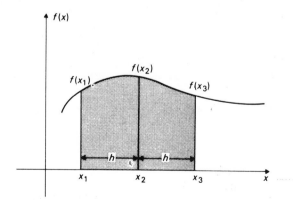

Fig. 13.2. Illustrating Simpson's rule.

UNIT 14
Working with tables

1 Introduction

The concept of a list, which is an array with one subscript, was introduced in Unit 10. Once the basic idea of using subscripts has been mastered, it is possible to move on to arrays with two subscripts. These are of great importance in computation. Programmers sometimes find that dealing with two subscripts does not come easily, so a careful approach to this Unit is advisable.

2 Tables and subscripts

All versions of BASIC will allow arrays to have one or two subscripts. Many versions also permit three or more. It has already been seen that with one subscript a list is formed, such as

$$A(1)$$
$$A(2)$$
$$A(3)$$

The extension to two subscripts is straightforward enough. A variable with two subscripts forms a table, such as

$C(1,1)$	$C(1,2)$	$C(1,3)$
$C(2,1)$	$C(2,2)$	$C(2,3)$
$C(3,1)$	$C(3,2)$	$C(3,3)$

The BASIC representation includes both subscripts, separated by a comma. The order of the subscripts should be noted; the first gives a row number and the second is the column number.

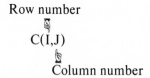

Row number
$$C(I,J)$$
Column number

In a similar way it is possible to use more subscripts, if a particular implementation of BASIC permits it.

Any variable which is used with subscripts is automatically recognised by BASIC to be an array. Now that both lists and tables are available it is necessary to be consistent in a program about the number of subscripts used with variable names. Once a list, always a list. Once a table, always a table. If no DIM statement is given, the largest possible subscript is taken to be 10. The form of the DIM statement should be generalised slightly:

line number DIM *variable* $\begin{pmatrix} integer \\ sizes, \\ commas \\ between \end{pmatrix}$, *variable* $\begin{pmatrix} integer \\ sizes \\ commas \\ between \end{pmatrix}$, ...

The variable can be a string constant or an ordinary variable.

Example

```
3Ø DIM Q$(23),Z(25,4Ø)
```

defines a string list Q$ with up to 23 entries and an ordinary table Z with 25 rows and 40 columns.

As with arrays of one dimension, the smallest subscript might be 0 or it might be 1. To make a program work on every BASIC, assume that it is 1.

Example   This subroutine will search a table with two subscripts for the largest value. The table is called T, and its first subscript is searched from 1 to T1, its second from 1 to T2. It returns to you with T3 and T4 telling you where the largest value is, and T5 is the value in question. T6 and T7 are used in the search.

```
2ØØØ REM SUBROUTINE WHICH SEARCHES FROM T(1,1)
2Ø1Ø REM TO T(T1,T2) FOR THE LARGEST VALUE
2Ø2Ø REM T(T3,T4) WHICH IS RETURNED IN T5
2Ø3Ø REM T6 AND T7 ARE USED FOR SEARCHING
2Ø4Ø REM INITIALISE − T(1,1) MIGHT BE IT
2Ø5Ø LET T5=T(1,1)
2Ø6Ø LET T3=1                        2Ø9Ø FOR T6=1 TO T1
2Ø7Ø LET T4=1                        21ØØ    FOR T7=1 TO T2
2Ø8Ø REM NOW SEARCH THE WHOLE  211Ø        IF T(T6,T7)<=T5 THEN 216Ø
                                     212Ø        REM HERE IS A BIGGER ONE
                                     213Ø        LET T5=T(T6,T7)
                                     214Ø        LET T3=T6
                                     215Ø        LET T4=T7
                                     216Ø    NEXT T7
                                     217Ø NEXT T6
                                     218Ø RETURN
```

3   Calculating with tables

Lists and tables are dealt with in much the same way, but in working with tables the demands on the thought processes can be more severe in keeping track of the rows and columns.

Suppose a company has four products and four branch offices. A record of sales figures for a particular quarter is kept in table form:

Containers plc

Branch

		London	Manchester	Liverpool	Birmingham
	Bottles	43	96	53	331
Product	Bags	600	143	270	201
	Boxes	215	400	311	192
	Bibelots	307	351	492	331

In a BASIC program DATA statements could be used to store the names of the cities and the products and also to save the table of values:

```
1Ø DATA 43,96,51,331
2Ø DATA 6ØØ,143,27Ø,2Ø1
3Ø DATA 215,4ØØ,311,192
4Ø DATA 3Ø7,351,492,331
5Ø DATA "LONDON","MANCHESTER","LIVERPOOL","BIRMINGHAM"
6Ø DATA "BOTTLES","BAGS","BOXES","BIBELOTS"
```

For convenience each row is written in one DATA statement, although there is nothing wrong with compressing the information into fewer statements. The data can be read into the table T in the following way:

```
1ØØ FOR I=1 TO 4        13Ø NEXT J
11Ø FOR J=1 TO 4        14Ø NEXT I
12Ø READ T(I,J)
```

Note carefully that the data has been read across the row by making the column number J increase most rapidly. I and J are popular variables to use as row and column numbers.

It is known from earlier work how string lists can be set up:

```
17Ø FOR K=1 TO 4
18Ø READ A$(K)          21Ø READ B$(K)
19Ø NEXT K              22Ø NEXT K
2ØØ FOR K=1 TO 4
```

After this has been done, A$ has the city names corresponding to the columns. B$ on the other hand is different from the others because it is organised to coincide with the rows and this will be important later.

Now that the table has been set up it can be calculated in various ways. First of all the rows are inspected to see how each commodity fares in the various cities. For each product the total sales and the best city are found:

```
300 FOR I=1 TO 4
310 LET S=0
320 LET M=0
330 FOR J=1 TO 4
340 LET S=S+T(I,J)
350 IF T(I,J)<M THEN 380
360 LET M=T(I,J)
370 LET M$=A$(J)
380 NEXT J
390 PRINT "WE HAVE SOLD ";S;B$(I)
400 PRINT "WE DID BEST IN ";M$;" WHERE WE SOLD ";M;B$(I)
410 NEXT I
```

Exercise Put this program together and run it. Improve the presentation.

4 Problems

Problem 14.1 All the products of Containers plc are sold in cases of value $1, and the data given are in cases. Process the columns to find out the total value of sales for each city and which product earned the most in that city.

Problem 14.2 Shuffle the table of Containers plc by program so that the cities and products are in alphabetical order. Print the table, with headings, in this form.

Problem 14.3 Shuffle the table by program so that the cities are in order of greatest total sales there and the products are also in order of greatest total sales in all cities. Print the table, with headings, in this form.

Problem 14.4 Write a story writing program using a table in which column 1 is an adjective, column 2 is a noun, column 3 a verb, column 4 an adverb, column 5 another adjective and column 6 a noun. Ask 6 friends each to type in 10 words to fill one column without consulting the others. Print the story. Then shuffle each column into alphabetical order and print this as Chapter 2. Some people have used computers to write music in a similar fashion—it too is sometimes pretty funny.

APPENDIX

A summary of basic BASIC

This summary describes a universal subset of BASIC which conforms to the ANSI X3.60-1978 and ECMA-55 1978 standards for minimal BASIC which are compatible with each other. Many systems will support facilities not described here, including additional commands, additional functions, and file manipulation statements.

1 BASIC programs

A program in BASIC consists of numbered statements, or lines, of the form

line number statement

Example

        1Ø PRINT 5/7
        2Ø END

When a BASIC program is executed, using the command RUN, the statements are obeyed in order of their line numbers unless the program itself dictates otherwise. The last line of every BASIC program must be an END statement.

2 Commands

Although commands are not covered by the standards, every BASIC system should support at least the following three commands, or some equivalent:

(i)   RUN—the current BASIC program is executed
(ii) LIST—the current BASIC program is printed at the terminal or screen
(iii) NEW—the current BASIC program is lost so that a new one may be commenced.

3 Creating BASIC programs

Although the interactive interface to BASIC is not covered by the standards, editing by line numbers is universally used. All keyboard entries to an interactive BASIC system, except when a program is running, will be interpreted as statements if a line begins with a number. Otherwise they will be interpreted as commands.

(a) *Entering* Programs are entered by typing each line with a line number and ending with the 'RETURN' key. (Unit 1)

(b) *Correcting* A line is replaced by typing the replacement in full, including the line number and the 'RETURN' key. (Unit 1)

(c) *Correcting lines while typing* There will be a symbol which eliminates the character before it. This might be backspace, delete, back arrow, or even CTRL and H. (Unit 1)

(d) *Inserting* A new line is inserted between two others by the use of a suitable line number. (Unit 1)

(e) *Deleting* A line is deleted by typing the line number and 'RETURN'. (Unit 1)

4   Numbers in BASIC

Numbers in BASIC can be expressed in three forms:

(a) Integer—a number written without a decimal point, e.g. 123.
(b) A number written with a decimal point, e.g. 3.1416.
(c) Exponential—a number written with an exponential indicated by the letter E, e.g. 1E10 means 1×10^{10}. (Unit 3)

5   Variables in BASIC

(a) Ordinary variables which represent numeric values in BASIC can be assigned any of 286 names which are the single letters:

A, B, C, . . . Z

or any letter plus a single digit:

A0, A1, . . . A9
B0, B1, . . . B9
Z0, Z1, . . . Z9   (Unit 3)

(b) String variables are identified by the 26 names:

A\$, B\$, . . . Z\$ (Unit 11)

(c) Ordinary variables
An ordinary variable is written without a subscript and it represents a single numerical value, e.g. X7.

(d) Arrays

A variable is an array or list if it is written with up to two subscripts, in which case it represents a list of values, e.g. Q$(9), N(I,J). An array must always have the same number of subscripts. Many versions of BASIC allow additional subscripts. (Units 10 and 14)

(e) Subscripts

A subscript can be any arithmetic expression; however the resulting value must be between the minimum and the maximum array size. Non-integer subscripts are truncated to integers. (Unit 10)

(f) Minimum subscripts

The minimum subscript should be 0, but on some systems it is 1. If the system conforms to the BASIC standard the minimum can be set by the statement OPTION BASE 0 or 1. However many systems do not conform and will not recognise OPTION. The safest thing is to regard 1 as the minimum. (Unit 10)

(g) Array sizes

The maximum size of an array is set up by the DIM statement, or by default to 10 in each subscript if no DIM statement is given. This means that if the minimum subscript is 0, arrays not set up by DIM statements have 11 possible subscripts (0 to 10). An array with one subscript will then have 11 members, while an array of two subscripts will have 121.

If the minimum subscript is 1, there are 10 possible subscripts unless a DIM statement is used. Arrays of one and two subscripts will have 10 and 100 members respectively.

6   Character string constants

(a) String constants are sequences of symbols usually enclosed in double quotation marks, e.g. "HELLO SAILOR". They may be used in the PRINT statement (Unit 1). They are also allowed in DATA, IF . . . THEN, and on the right hand side of the LET statement. (Unit 11)

(b) String variables have any of the 26 names A$, B$, . . . Z$. They may be used in the statements INPUT, PRINT, READ, IF . . . THEN, LET and DIM (and so may be subscripted). (Unit 11)

(c) In comparing strings using the IF . . . THEN statement, the standard only supports tests of equality or non-equality. However most implementations treat strings nearer the beginning of the alphabet as less than those nearer the end. (Unit 11)

For example

"AB" is less than "AC"
"AB" is less than "ABA"

7 Arithmetic expressions

BASIC uses the hierarchy of operators

( )	expressions in brackets	high priority
$\wedge$	exponentiation	
* /	multiplication and division	
+ $-$	addition and subtraction	low priority

The result of an expression is always as if operations of equal priority are performed from left to right. Arithmetic expressions may be written involving these operations and any variables or constants, e.g. $(A+3)/D(I)$.

A single variable or constant is itself a valid expression.

Two operators may not appear together, e.g. $A+-B$ is not allowed. Operators normally separate two values, e.g. 3*B, but the operator $-$ has 'unary' meaning, e.g. $-J$ or $3*(-B)$. (Unit 2)

8 Relational expressions

(a) Relational expressions are written

arithmetic   relational   arithmetic
expression   operator   expression

for example

A > B

The result of the relational expression is TRUE or FALSE. Relational expressions are used in the IF . . . THEN statement. (Unit 5)

(b) The relational operators are

=	equal to	
>	greater than	
<	less than	
>=	greater than or equal to	
<=	less than or equal to	
<>	not equal to	(Unit 5)

(c) In some systems relational expressions can be more complicated, involving the additional operators AND and OR (inclusive) as in

(A<B*1∅) OR (C>=1)

(d) In some systems the results TRUE or FALSE have the values 1 and 0 and can be used as part of any arithmetic expression.

(e) The string relational expression is available for the operations of equality or non-equality ($<>$). Usually systems will allow any comparison.

> *string   relational   string*
> *operator*

for example

   "ABC">=B$(I)   (Unit 11)

9   Library functions

All BASIC systems should support the following set of library functions:

Function   Meaning

SIN(x)   The sine of x where x is an angle in radians.
COS(x)   The cosine of x where x is in radians.
TAN(x)   The tangent of x where x is in radians.
ATN(x)   The arctangent of an angle x in the range $-\pi/2$ to $+\pi/2$ radians.
EXP(x)   The value of e^x.
LOG(x)   The natural logarithm of x.
ABS(x)   The absolute value of x.
SQR(x)   The square root of x.
INT(x)   The largest integer not greater than x. For example, INT(5.95)$=$5 and INT(-5.95)$=-6$.
SGN(x)   The sign of x; has value 1 if x is positive, 0 if x is 0, or -1 if x is negative.

In the above functions, x represents any expression, which may of course include other functions. The quantity x is called the argument or parameter of the function. (Unit 6)

The function RND, which is a random number generator, appears in most versions of BASIC. It does not always have an argument—if it does, the argument may not have a meaning.

The TAB function is a special function associated with the PRINT statement, as described in Section 11 of this Appendix.

10   The statements of basic BASIC

The statements of BASIC are summarised here in alphabetical order. Items in square brackets are optional.

line number DATA *constant, constant, . . .*

> The *constants* given in the DATA statement are stored in the computer in the order given. Successive DATA statements add to the list in order. Information in the list is assigned to variables by the READ statement. (Unit 12)

> Strings can be defined in the DATA statement. It is recommended that the quotation marks should always be given because the arrangement suggested by the standard on this issue is not followed by most systems.

> For example

> DATA "STRING","STRING+31" (Unit 11)

line number DEF FN*a*(*variable*) = *expression*

> This statement is used for function definition. See Section 12 of this Appendix. (Unit 9)

line number DIM *subscripted variable, subscripted variable, . . .*

> The DIM statement specifies the maximum size of arrays. In the DIM statement the subscripts must be integer numbers. If an array is not mentioned in a DIM statement, the maximum is 10 in each subscript. The standard recommends that one or two subscripts should be allowed, but many versions of BASIC will allow more. (Unit 10)

line number END

> The END statement must be the last in any BASIC program, i.e. it must be present and have the highest line number. When it is encountered the execution of a BASIC program terminates. (Unit 1)

> To terminate a program before the highest line number, the STOP statement is used. (Unit 13)

line number FOR *variable* = *expression a* TO *expression b* [STEP *expression c*]

> The FOR statement begins a FOR . . . NEXT program loop, which is repeated with the named *variable* having the initial value given by *expression a* and changing by *expression c* until *expression b* is reached. The word STEP and *expression c* are optional, and if not given the step is taken as 1. The named

variable can be adjusted during the loop, but the initial, final, and step values are fixed when the loop first begins and cannot later be changed. A loop may be jumped over altogether if these values suggest that it should, for example in

```
FOR I=1∅ TO 1 STEP 1
```

A program must not jump into loops from outside. The end of a loop is indicated by a NEXT statement, which must be present. FOR . . . NEXT loops using different variables may be nested. (Unit 7)

line number a GOSUB *line number b*

This statement is used to call a subroutine. See Section 12 of this Appendix. (Unit 13)

line number a GO TO *line number b*

The GO TO statement causes a jump to *line number b*. (Unit 4)

line number a IF r*elational expression* THEN *line number b*

When the IF statement is encountered, the *relational expression* is evaluated and if it is TRUE, then the program jumps to *line number b*. If the *relational expression* is FALSE, the execution continues from the next line after *line number a*. (Unit 5)

line number INPUT *variable, variable, . . .*

The INPUT statement causes the computer to request information by displaying a prompting symbol, usually ?, and waiting until a line of information is entered.

Exactly the correct number of quantities should be entered, separated by commas. If the wrong number of values is given, standard BASICs should require all of it to be entered again. In any event the message given by the computer should be clear.

line number LET *variable = expression*

In the LET statement the *expression* on the right hand side is evaluated and the result replaces the value of the *variable* on the left hand side. (Unit 3)

line number NEXT *variable*

The NEXT statement identifies the end of the FOR . . . NEXT loop in which the *variable* was the one used in the FOR statement. (Unit 7) *line number a* ON *expression* GO TO *line number b, line number c, . . .*

The ON . . . GO TO statement allows a multiple choice of branches to the destinations given in *line number b, line number c, ...* The *expression* is evaluated and truncated to an integer. If the result is 1, the program jumps to *line number b*, if 2 to *line number c*, and so on. If the *expression* is negative, zero, or too large for the number of destinations given, an error message is produced. (Unit 5)

line number OPTION BASE 0 *or* 1

This statement tells a system whether the minimum subscript for arrays is to be 0 or 1. Most current versions of BASIC will not recognise this. The safest thing it to regard the minimum subscript as 1. (Unit 6)

line number PRINT *quantity separator quantity separator . . .*

This statement produces printed output. See Section 12 of this Appendix.

line number RANDOMIZE

Selects an apparently random starting place for the RND function. (Unit 10)

line number READ *variable, variable, . . .*

The READ statement assigns values to the named *variable*s from the list defined by DATA statements. As successive READ statements are encountered, they continue through the DATA list until they are satisfied. The *variable*s may be string variables. (Unit 12)

line number REM *any remark or comment*

The REM statement has no effect on the execution of a BASIC program, and is provided to allow remarks to be inserted to explain the program. (Unit 3)

line number RESTORE

The RESTORE statement returns subsequent READ statements to the beginning of the DATA list. (Unit 12)

line number RETURN

This statement is used in subroutines. See Section 12 of this Appendix. (Unit 13)

line number STOP

This statement terminates the execution of a program and is used when a program is to stop before the last line (which is the END statement). (Unit 13)

11   Printing

All BASIC systems support the PRINT statement:

line number PRINT *quantity separator quantity separator . . .*

where *quantity* can be

(a)   an expression resulting in numerical output
(b)   a character string in quotation marks resulting in literal output
(c)   a string variable resulting in literal output
(d)   the TAB function

and *separator* can be a comma or semicolon, as explained below.

A PRINT statement starts a new line unless a final separator was explicitly given in the previous PRINT, in which case it continues on the same line.

A PRINT statement containing more items than can be printed on a line will be continued on the following line.

The *comma*   The print line is divided into typically 5 zones of 15 spaces. The comma causes the next quantity to be printed beginning in the first space of the next zone.

The *semicolon* between quantities causes the output to be compressed. After a TAB function or a character string printing continues in the next space. Between numerical output the spacing depends on the numbers but at least one space should be given after (but not before) numbers. At the end of a PRINT statement the semicolon causes the next PRINT statement to continue on the same line.

Numbers may appear in the printed output as integers, or as numbers with decimal places, or in exponential format.

The TAB function TAB(*expression*) may appear as a quantity in a PRINT statement. This causes the printer to move forward to the column number given by the integer part of the *expression*. If asked to move backwards or beyond the end of a line, it will move to an appropriate column in the next line.

12   Functions and subroutines

(a) *Functions*   (Unit 9)

All BASIC systems support the single line function definition:

   line number DEF FN*a* (*variable*) = *expression*

a can be the letters A through Z; thus the 26 names FNA, FNB, . . . FNZ are available.
The standard for BASIC does not provide for string functions, but most implementations
do allow A$ to Z$ as additional names of string functions.

When a function name is implicitly used in a running program, the *expression* on the
right hand side is evaluated using the given value of the function *variable*. The function
variable is thus a 'dummy' for the value used while running, and should be of the correct
type (ordinary variable or string variable).

Only one definition of a particular function should be used. Functions may use other
functions, but not themselves and endless loops may not be established.

(b) *Subroutines*   (Unit 13)

Subroutines are called by the GOSUB statement:

   line number a GOSUB *line number b*

The running program continues from *line number b* until a RETURN is encountered,
when it carries on from the line after *line number a*. Subroutines may call other
subroutines but not themselves and loops may not be so established.

Subroutines are ended by the RETURN statement:

   line number RETURN

The running program returns to the line after the latest GOSUB.

The STOP statement terminates program execution:

   line number STOP

Index